So Good, So Far...

So Good, So Far...

Grady Nutt

impact
books

Nashville, Tennessee

OTHER BOOKS BY GRADY NUTT:

Being Me (Broadman)
The Gospel According to Norton (Broadman)
Agaperos (Broadman)

Library of Congress Catalog Card Number: 79-90248

ISBN 0-914850-53-9
M0510

DEDICATION

To Lewis Wilson—
      my father-in-law . . .
        the best
        and most honest man
        I've ever known;
And to Frances Wilson—
      my mother-in-law . . .
        the most
        mature person
        I've ever met.
Together they
      believed in me
        when they could have
        doubted . . .
      supported me
        when they could have
        criticized . . .
      taught me
        to love
        by unselfish/unqualified
        example . . .
      called out of me
        every good gift
        they ever saw.
And they taught all that
      to Eleanor—
        their daughter,
        my wife—
      and she worked my puzzle!

TABLE OF CONTENTS

BEFORE-WORDS
by Ralph Edwards

I sat down to read the manuscript of this book in the shadow of a large pine tree 9,000 feet up in the Rocky Mountains above the rushing waters of the White River. I finished it in my home in Beverly Hills. I was not distracted by either setting.

I had expected to find a series of humorous episodes molded in the well known Grady Nutt story-telling tradition. It was that, alright, plus ten times more. The author's humor ranges from wry to hilarious, of course. But, make no mistake about it, there are two sides to the man. From birth, Grady Nutt seemed to have two commitments. One was to the ministry; the other, to the field of entertainment—somewhat like two strong trees sharing the same trunk.

Grady is so overwhelming as a performer that I had forgotten he is also an ordained minister. As he unfolded his life in as honest a fashion as any biographer ever has, it became increasingly apparent that this was not an entertainer doing a stock exposé of his life. This was a masterpiece of introspection, intelligently written, finely honed—a step-by-step dissection of a man's mind and soul. Here was anguish and love and high humor. A book with great value for readers of all ages.

I first met Grady twelve years ago at a nationwide meeting of University Alumni Directors in San Francisco. I was producing a television program involving students and alumni of our American universities. A friend from the University of California arranged for me to be on the agenda to explain my TV show and its mechanics to those alumni directors whom I would be contacting. He said I would follow a fellow named Grady Nutt.

"What's a Grady Nutt?" I asked.

"He is an alumni director," he said, "but a really good entertainer. Wait until you hear him!"

Well, hear him I did. As I listened while Grady brought rocket-bursts of laughter from his peers, I wished to myself that: (a) I had gone on earlier in the program rather than follow this show-stealer; (b) beefed up my presentation a bit more, or (c) never asked my friend to book me in the first place!

I was tremendously impressed, but I'll let you read what Grady has to say about that experience in his own words. Whatever my peripheral association with Grady has been through the years, after reading *So Good, So Far,* I realized I never knew the real Grady Nutt at all. I liked him before. I admire him now.

Grady's text wears as well as a favorite shirt that's been through the wringer more than once. It is both interesting and fulfilling for me to see in Grady Nutt, author, another dimension of the man and the things he believes in so deeply.

Up to now, much of what we have heard and read concerning Inside-America religion, particularly that of an evangelistic nature, has been treated in some quarters as a kind of charade, a fanatical approach to a higher land. This author will please the many millions who cherish the Golden Rule, the Parables, the Beatitudes, the Ten Commandments, and the warmth of the spirit that came with the Sunday night service.

There are many high points in this book. I'll point out just two of them. The chapter entitled "The Unmasking Marvel" should be read by all troubled married couples. "Follow the Leader, But Watch Your Step" is a great lesson in psychology if you dare to compare your own shortcomings. And the last chapter is, in effect, a sermon. This wit, this funny storyteller is, after all, a minister—no matter what he says . . .

I take this opportunity to commend Grady and his wife, Eleanor, for working out the complexities of his life. I invite you to share the rewards of this extraordinary autobiography.

RALPH EDWARDS
BEVERLY HILLS, CALIFORNIA

INTRODUCTION:
or, Why I took almost a year of my life to write this book!

Greetings, reader . . .

Should you choose to wade on into the book you now "toe-dip" in your hands and in your curiosity, I will then promise to lead you with precision and care over a course I know well. Better than anyone.

My good friend, Roger Ray, once conjured up a terrific sermon title that I don't believe ever got a sermon under it. The title: "Up A Mountain Without A Guide." The mountain I want you to climb with me is one I know well. I am the only qualified guide. The mountain is my life.

So far . . .

I'd like to take you to, over, around, inside and all about it. I will try to make you aware of things you'd never notice without my expert services as guide.

This is not really an autobiography. It is surely not an "ought to" biography. Nothing about my life screams out to be told. If you *never* read this—as millions will *not*—your life will still probably have meaning.

This is basically *witness*. And *witness* is the only word that will work here. It is *my* witness. *My* observations. *My* testimony. It is "one beggar telling another beggar where he found bread . . ."

Witness. Wit with a purpose. Wit as a gift. Wit as servant. Wit as tool. Wit as cup; truth as broth. Parable going somewhere, on mission. I have been blessed with a witty heritage, funny ancestors/parents/family. My life, with the very special folks I thank in this book, has been unfolding more and more as a gift. The fun I find in life has been pointed out to me, modeled for me, ingrained into me. It has been done wittingly; it has been done wittily.

I am convinced that Christian witness, testimony, should always be a "progress report." It should be a state of the union; better still, a state of the "communion." It should reflect what has gone on *so far.* It should describe how it has been to this point. This will be that kind of testimony.

I will be frank and honest. I'll tease your eyes with the printed page and your mind with my own brand of insight and ask you to play leapfrog through the joyful people of my past and present. I'll take you where I've been.

Roger Ray had one sermon title that finally did attract a super sermon. Title: "Looking in the Back of the Book for the Answers." He said: "You can't look in the back of the book with your life like you could when you were in fourth-grade arithmetic and wanted to be sure that seven-times-eight was really and truly fifty-six." He's right. You have to test the footing, blaze your own trail, slip, camp with ideas and folks, travel. For your witness to be honest, you have to give a progress report.

All of us are in transit. Right now I am looking out the window of Continental Airlines Flight 80. I'm watching New Mexico move by 37,000 feet and some snow below. I am watching an autumn sun ease up on the desert for the night so it can catch its breath for another dry day tomorrow. The flight attendant said just moments ago that we'll land in El Paso, Texas, in twenty minutes. I certainly hope so! But, for now, seventy-six of us are *in transit*. Continental-willing, we will hit the land of the tamale shortly. Or, as they say: *poquito*.

My witness to you is only partly *places* and *itinerary*. It is largely *persons* who have laid hands on my soul and life to bless me. I've spent "a heap of time as a heap for a time" in some very real ditches. I have been passed by on the other side by folks with "temple" kinds of things to do. I am who/what/whatever I am today because of the Samaritans who have oiled my wounds and donkeyed me to help. Typically good Samaritans, they did not count the cost (and I cannot adequately repay!). They never asked to be known or noticed, never used their concern as leverage or pressure on me. I can stand more nearly straight and tall because they stooped to help me. Like blind Bartemaeus, "Now I see."

Hence, the title of this monumental work: *So Good, So Far . . . I* know I am not immune to problems, hurt, pain, and disaster. Rain does fall on the just and the unjust, though we tend to think it falls *just on the just*! Here you will read the confessions of a happy, fortunate, *former* ditchdweller! It is not hard to figure out where I'd be without all those who helped me out of the ditches. I know!

I've been there . . .

GRADY NUTT
LOUISVILLE, KENTUCKY

A SHOOT OUT OF THE STUMP OF A DIFFERENT JESSE

I was born at the Nutt house.

True! It was located at 13th and Roberts on the east side of Amarillo, Texas. It was operated by my parents—Grady and Doris Nutt.

I was born at home. Right in the house. The doctor made house calls. That fact will tell you that I was born before World War II. And right after the Great Depression. Talk about timing!

The Nutt house was small. The streets were dirt. You had to walk four blocks to a paved one. The houses were painted by dwellers one year, sandblasted by the Texas wind the next.

Natives of the plains have the same unpainted, windcarved look about them . . .

I was only half Nutt. The other half was Rickman. It still is. Mom's parents—Nellie and Jesse Rickman—lived five or six blocks away, just past the Sanborn Elementary School on East Sixth Street. You could walk it in about ten minutes and had to cross only one busy street. It was the paved one.

I was the firstborn of fourborn. I was also the oldest grandchild. I loved having a head start on the other grandchildren at spending time with my grandparents. *Grand* is really appropriate for them.

There is a verse in the Bible: "There shall come forth a shoot from the stump of Jesse, and a branch shall grow out of his roots . . ." (Isa. 11:1, RSV). I found that verse when I was about twelve and thought for a moment it was talking about me! I was rooted in the affection and love of Jesse Rickman; my shoots were his kinds of shoots. Most of this booksworth of memory is out of his kind of soil . . .

He was a natural and likable wit, last one to get a wise word in edgewise. Practical joker, never impractical. Warm, approachable, happy. Grandma was a jovial counterpart and counterpoint to his personality. They were proud of their family. Four children—three boys and a girl. In order, they were: Noel, Doris (my mom), Leroy, and Jesse Coleman Rickman, Jr.—called "Junior" at home, "J.C." at school or on dates.

I grew up around all of them. At one time the entire family lived within about an eight-block radius. We "frontporched" it, had occasional Sunday dinner together, shared the holiday times, and knew each other well. Every one of the family inherited Granddad's love for fun.

Noel always loved horses. He kept a couple of palomino ponies out back of his house *right in town.* The neighbors didn't seem to mind. Horse and horse smell just seemed to be the ultimate in West Texas basics. After oil.

Noel was also the "checker champion of the world." He told me so. He also told me he never lied. I was at least "all-hemisphere," but I never beat him even once! He taught me all I know about checkers. And losing. And drawing horses. I still draw them like he taught me. Most folks can see one of my sketches and say right off: "It's a horse!" I give Noel credit for that particular skill.

The next child born to the Rickmans was my mom. Tough to be raised in a family of pranksters and brothers. She held her own and gave it back in multiples! More about her later . . .

Next was Leroy. He was only about five feet, three inches tall and weighed about one-hundred-five pounds. And that's when he *jumped* on the scales! He had suffered polio as a child and was crippled a bit in one leg. Maybe that's why he was such a scrapper and why he was called "Buster." He could "bust" just about anyone. Stories about his "giant-slaying" were as popular as David and Goliath.

I wanted to be like Buster because of the "Put and Take" gang. We lived down the street from the "Put and Take Grocery." Mom would occasionally send me to the store for small orders. I'd go gladly so I could read the latest comics and *Jack and Jill Magazine*. The grocery got its name from a practice intended to end credit to customers: You had to "put" down your money before you could "take" out your groceries! The "Put and Take" gang, as I called them, were a bunch of neighborhood ruffians who tried to catch me and steal my money on the way to the store. I imagined myself being able to handle things like my rough-and-tough Uncle Buster. I usually got busted, though . . .

J. C., or "Junior," was seven years older than I. He is still more nearly my big brother than my mom's little one. He is the first in a long line of idols and ideals for me. I saw in him all the things I wanted to be—good-looking, fun, popular, tall, *older*. I'm sure I must have "pestered" him to death, but he was patient and proud of me. I used to go to my grandparents' home in the afternoon to take naps on Junior's bed . . .

Mom must have felt like a Texan at the Alamo—
outnumbered but not outdone! She was equally as
witty and crafty as her brothers. She was the life of
virtually every party. She was attractive and outgoing
and funny.

And she was musical. Very musical. After school
she used to tend to the needs of an invalid lady. The
lady had an old upright piano. My mom would sit
and pick out tunes, primarily church songs, and
taught herself to play the piano by ear. As she
progressed in her skills, she also began to pick up
basic music instruction in public school. By the time
she was fifteen or sixteen years old, she could play
almost any tune she could see or hear—and she had
never taken a lesson! This talent made her the center
of attention.

I believe this is how she must have attracted my
Dad. He was a rangy, big-boned "farm boy come to
town" who had moved to Amarillo during the
Depression years. After several short-term jobs, he
landed a position with the Borden's Milk Company
in Amarillo, where he was to work for fourteen
years. He started on the routes, selling milk to
individual customers, ice for their boxes at home,
other dairy products as needed.

He never met a stranger. He had a salesman's gift
for getting back into your life on a regular basis. He
moved into Mom's life permanently! They married
when she was nineteen and he was twenty. I was
born in the second year of their marriage.

My parents had it very tough in those early years.
Just about everyone did then. We were stretched
quite thin financially. Dad's take-home pay after
fourteen-hour days was about sixteen dollars per
week. It costs more than that now for a tank of gas!

Much of my frustration with Dad later in life grew

out of the fact that all his life he had to work so hard he never learned to play. As soon as he was old enough, he was working on the farm. Instead of playing with cast-iron trucks and toys, he was shin-whipped by roots as he followed a mule and plow over unproductive, stubborn soil. He left school in the eighth grade at age sixteen, to battle the scrub-infected, low-yield farm, and then to leave home for good.

My playfulness has always been a mystery to him, it seems to me . . .

My playfulness was no mystery to Jesse Rickman! He was the grandfather of playfulness! He helped me celebrate the wonder and fascination of childhood so that when I grew up I decided never to quit being a child!

The flashbacks of my time in the old neighborhood are in vivid technicolor. I recall our collie, Rusty, getting poisoned by a crank neighbor. I remember finding a rattlesnake in our front yard one afternoon. Mom killed it with a garden hoe in the key of high C! It was longer than she was tall.

I remember throwing darts back and forth across the street with Huey Davis and having one lodge painfully in my shin. I remember licorice and B.B. Bats and Fleers Bubble Gum. I remember not knowing I was poor.

Nothing do I remember as vividly from my childhood as being around the home of my grandparents. I was asked in a conference one time to think on the word *warmth* for a few moments and then suggest what it brought to mind. I immediately said: "My grandparents!" (I never knew Dad's parents. His father died when I was about eighteen months old; his mother died when I was fourteen. I think I only saw her four or five times in my life.)

My Grandma Rickman was small, bordering on
tiny. I think Leroy got all her "small." She was gray
by the time she was thirty, so I'm told. For sheer
warmth, she is the Franklin Stove of my memory.
Not a scolder. Affectionate. She let us stay up later
than my folks would; she let me rummage through
special desk drawers; she let me keep treasures
hidden in secret places around the house and in the
garage.

She loved me dearly and clearly. She made
fantastic hot rolls, cooked buckwheat pancakes
whenever I spent the night. She was the first adult I
outgrew!

My grandfather was the joyful center of the
Rickman clan. He was the happy man, the laughing
man. He could have tubs of fun without putting you
down or making you *feel* put down.

The preeminent family man, he provided for a
wife and four kids by working as an engineer for the
Santa Fe Railroad. Once he let me sit in his lap at
the roundhouse in one of the big steam engines. He
showed me how to pull the cord or chain—can't
remember which—that made the steam whistle blow.
Sitting in his lap and doing delightful things was
typical of the ten years I had with him before he
died.

Mostly, I remember the stories he told and the
way he told them. He could find something funny in
a traffic ticket! I loved the times when our table talk
was combined with tall tales. I sat and listened to
him and the other menfolk tell about special teams of
horses they had used to pull heavy loads. I heard
about crossing flooded rivers with wagonloads of
very little that was valuable, and yet it was all they
owned. There were stories of barn accidents, fast
horses, cows that could really give milk, pranks

pulled in school, courting and "sparking" tales, and
heavy load-lifters that made Samson look like
Truman Capote! Of all the storytellers, Granddad
was the champ. Whenever he started an episode,
even the Texas wind hushed to listen . . .

I was the oldest grandchild, but I did not take to
most of the games the other children wanted to play.
I think it was really because I was afraid I'd miss out
on a tale or two about a relative, a fast horse, or a
flooded river! I sat at the table in awe and
amazement as the stories unfurled and billowed
around me.

Occasionally, I threw in one of my own. I'd tell
about a big scuffle on the school grounds, about a
narrow escape from the "Put-and-Take" gang, about
a large dog I had scared, or a snake that nearly got
me and my hoe-swinging mom! They always
listened. They always laughed. They included me in
the circle of the storytellers.

Just as my mom played the piano by ear, I played
my audience of turkey-and cranberry sauce-
devourers "without lessons." They responded to me
like the keyboard responded to her touch . . .

When I was seven years old, my granddad had a
stroke. I had never heard of one. All I knew was that
everyone looked very serious, even at the table.
Tones were low. I'd let the group in on the latest
alley war or dog dodge, and they'd "shush" me. I
was puzzled. I knew my granddad was in the
hospital, but that wasn't serious. That was where you
got babies.

They brought him home to lie in bed for a long
time. He was partially paralyzed on one side. His
face was drawn on that side, cheek hanging like cake
icing in a warm room. His speech was slow and a bit
thick, tripping over his nearly dead lip on the way

out. My keenest memory of all that was that my happy grandfather couldn't laugh anymore, so none of the family did, either.

But he got better. Before too long he could sit up in a rocker. Later he could get around on an oak walking cane, dragging his nearly useless foot along.

My grandma went to work at White's Laundry, about four walking blocks away. She made sure the right names were in the collars of white shirts and did other assorted tasks, including waiting on the counter when customers came for their freshly starched goods. My first job was staying with granddad after school.

I'd go over to his house and sit with him in the bedroom or run errands for him. About 3:30 each afternoon, I'd go into the living room and get a nickel off the starched doily under the Seth Thomas mantel clock. This was my salary for tending to my granddad's needs. The salary didn't last long!

I'd rush across the street to the little neighborhood grocery with the metal Holsum Bread sign across the door. The screen was badly "pooched" out, torn several inches' worth at the bottom. The floors had not seen varnish in years. They bore the smell and oily evidence of having been swept out with treated sawdust. I'd get one of two things: either an Eskimo pie (vanilla ice cream bar with chocolate "bark" on it) or a licorice stick (one inch in diameter, six inches long, corrugated). I'd dash back across the street and sit by my granddad's bed and listen to him tell stories about his youth—his horse-breaking days in New Mexico and Montana, his exploits with the Santa Fe Railroad. You couldn't pay an audience to give you that kind of attention! I'd sit there with licorice or Eskimo pie all over my shirt, listening so hard I'd forget to eat.

When he was really feeling chipper, he'd tell my favorite story . . .

It happened when he was living in the small mining town of Yankee, New Mexico. He hauled coal from the mines in a horse-drawn wagon down the mountain many miles to the railroad line. As part-time employment, he worked for the New Mexico Fish and Wildlife Commission, killing wildcats and mountain lions. That was the Fish and Wildlife's idea of environmental control! The bounties he collected on the trophies supplemented the family income somewhat.

It was a cold and snowy winter. Granddad was fighting a mountain roadful of snow with a loaded wagon. He made it as far as possible, then camped for the night. He ate his dinner from a tin pie plate, and then put it on the canvas-covered wagon. He led his horses down the slope into an evergreen thicket. They were hobbled and made ready for the night. Then he bedded down under the wagon which acted as his rooftop in case of more snow. The day had been hard and the bedroll was a welcome relief. Sleep came quickly.

About 3:00 a.m. he was awakened by the rattling of the tin pie plate atop the wagon under which he slept. *Coon? he wondered.* More rattling. *More wondering.* Louder rattling. *Large goosebumps.* A deep growl. *Terror!*

Slowly he pulled himself to the edge of the wagon and peered up into the moonlit winter night. On top of the wagon was a full-grown, card-carrying mountain lion! He was licking the pan to get at the leftover supper. In mid-lick, the lion heard something under the wagon. He leaned over, curious to see what was beneath him. Man and animal looked each other in the eye. The lion "squalled" and my granddad shouted/yelled! The lion sprang from the wagon horseward!

The hobbled horses were in a frenzy. I'm sure each of them was thinking: "I'll never pull a wagon again for a man who handcuffs you when the lions are out!" Pandemonium! Then, except for the cold, cloudy panting of coal hauler and horses, there was not another sound, and the silent forest embraced them once again.

The next morning, Granddad surveyed the footprints in the snow. He was shocked and startled by the size of the cat's feet and the span of his leaps in his getaway from the wagon.

The story was hair-raising. It always kept me on the edge of my seat, drippy Eskimo pie and all. As I look back on it in later years from a grown-up perspective, I can see now that each time he told that story, the night got colder, the snow got deeper, the lion got bigger, and he got braver!

Granddad wasn't lying. He was *storytelling*! Bill Cosby calls it "remembering big!" I remember it *very* big!

And I remember great stories *about* him.

One is a classic. He had worked all one Saturday morning planting his front yard in new grass seed. This was shortly after moving into the house where he eventually died. He had already made fast friends of all the waifs on the block. They called him "Uncle Jess." I remember that he looked just like an "Uncle Jess." In fact, if he hadn't been my grandfather, I'd probably have called him Uncle Jess, too.

He roughed up the barren soil, laid in some new seed, smoothed it all over with the back of the rake, then stood to admire his handiwork. He gathered up all the tools and sacks and yard paraphernalia and headed for the small garage. He put the stuff away

in the proper places, closed the wooden doors, and
laid in the crossbar that held them fast. With a look
of satisfaction, he headed around to the front to see
if any grass had sprouted yet!

In the time he had been cleaning up and putting
away the garden tools, his smooth lawn had been
scarred. Across the fresh dirt, seed a-germinating,
ran a set of bicycle tracks accompanied by a set of
bare footprints. Most folks would have gone looking
for a kid with grass seeds between his toes and in his
tire treads. Not Uncle Jess.

He made a U-turn, headed for the garage,
unbarred the door, got his rake and seed. With a
cheerful hum and near serenity he set to smoothing
and reseeding. It didn't take too long to repair the
damage.

Then he called Grandma and asked her to bring
him some kite twine and an old piece of bedsheet.
While she scurried about, he broke small limbs from
a mimosa tree and stuck them in the ground around
the new-sown seed patch. When Grandma returned,
he wound the kite twine around the tree limbs to
fence off the area. Then he tore the bedspread into
rags and tied them on the twine between the "tree
limb fence posts."

Back to the garage. Back in place with the rake,
the seedbag, etc. Back to the front yard to see that
he had the new grass sufficiently barricaded.
Satisfied, he called a neighborhood meeting.

The kids came running from all over East Sixth
Street to sit on the curb in front of the house at
1315.

There they were—seventeen runny-nosed "hopes
of the world." Granddad addressed them: "Fellows, I
need some help, and I want to see how many
helpers I can find. I want to find out how many of

you I can get to help me grow some grass seed."

They looked at him. They looked at each other. They looked puzzled. He explained further:

"Let me tell you what I need. See the patch where I've planted the new grass seed?"

They turned to look. You can *hear* seventeen kids turn to look!

"What I need is some help to keep people from walking on my new grass seed. Now, for everyone who agrees to help me, I have two requirements and a reward. *First*, I want you to help me by staying off the grass yourself. *Second*, I want you to help me by keeping other folks off the grass. For each helper, the day I can mow the grass for the first time and take down the little kite-twine fence, I'm going to make home-made ice cream (during the Depression, mind you!). Everyone who helps me gets all the home-made ice cream he can eat. Now, how many helpers do I have?"

Each kid voted with both hands. They were eager to help. And they *did* help! This happened before I was born, but Grandma and J.C. both told me those kids were an absolute *posse* in search of potential grass mashers! The next-door neighbor, Mrs. Smith, who accidentally stepped off the walk one day and got a small hunk of grass underfoot, was swarmed by seventeen young "runny-nosed hopes of the world" who were helping Uncle Jess grow grass!

From that story I learned one of my most lasting lessons from my mom's dad. He kept his cool and he got his grass! He believed that kids were more important than grass seed, and so he got his grass seed to grow. And he also proved another interesting fact: *When you love kids more than grass seed, a piece of kite twine will do a better job than a brick wall!* He built into them a desire to help him, not a fear of him.

At his bedside, in his lap on a train, trying to outeat him on the hot rolls at Thanksgiving, he made me feel so special for ten short years that I found a bedrock of joy, of giving and receiving affection, of loving kids with all my heart.

From all that I gained a love for storytelling, a sense of closeness to family that has made family the most important part of my life.

I was planted like a small acorn, sprouted with a sense of destiny and enthusiasm, gained first-leaves among strong models, and felt affirmation as strong as a kite-twine fence with bedsheet rags!

It was rooting time . . .

THE CRADLE ROCKED TO A GOSPEL BEAT

Life moves from roots to shoots.

I was rooted in the pleasant joy of Jesse Rickman's love for fun and family. He bequeathed a double portion to his second child, Doris. My mom.

She got all his wit and funny rolled up in a talented female package. She was a bright and winsome young woman, just the kind my dad would fall for! He really fell hard. She delighted him with her music, her good looks, her fun. And, I think, with her family.

Music. You cannot think of my mom as a young woman without thinking about music. She filled my early life with it. I attribute most of my love for performing to the environment she created with her singing and her piano playing. She pressured me to learn new songs and perform them for all kinds of church groups. I did not love some of the time I spent learning hymns instead of playing ball or riding a tricycle, but I did love the feeling of pleasing an audience.

I was performing for church groups when I was old enough to stand in a metal chair without wobbling. I had to get up in the chair to be seen by church supper crowds and to see over pulpits at Sunday afternoon singings. My mom could play any hymn you named—with a bit of permissible *jazzing.* The kind you *could* dance to but weren't *allowed* to!

We lived near the Tenth Street Methodist Church until I was about six years old. It was there that I first remember singing in church. I was about three years old. Mother would bring me in about mid-afternoon, stand me against the end of the upright piano, and teach me a hymn a day by rote. I knew over three hundred hymns by the time I was five years old, at least two verses each. I could sing them until tears would come to the eyes of a portrait!

My brother, Don, was born almost three years after I hit 13th and Roberts. He was roped into the family singing act, also. Mostly, he stood there and looked cute while I carried the main load. I had strict instructions from the folks: *Stand still, hands at your sides; don't look around; sing loud and clear; don't let anything distract you.*

One night, Don got the sillies!

We were singing in a small church in Amarillo, to a church-supper crowd, standing on a tabletop so we could be seen. I was about six; he was just past three. We were dressed identically in burgundy sailor suits trimmed in white; long, squared-at-the-bottom collars. We were wearing white sailor caps with our individual initials on the front of the turned-up bills.

The pants buttoned onto the shirttails. I was singing as instructed—straight ahead, hands at sides, loud and clear.

Don started clowning! He began unbuttoning my pants from my shirt! I was terrified! Straight ahead . . . *one button* . . . hands at side . . . *two buttons* . . . loud . . . *three*

buttons . . . clear . . . *four buttons* . . . don't let
anything distract you . . . *five buttons* . . . my dad
was standing against the back wall in
hysterics . . . *six buttons* . . . I had tears running
down my cheeks . . . *seven buttons* . . . he wouldn't
rescue me . . . DOWN THEY CAME!!

The audience was delirious! Mom was playing by
touch, because she couldn't see the keys for the
tears! I finally broke a rule and reached down and
pulled up my pants. I sang *every* note. I didn't let
anything distract me!

I nearly killed Don when we got home!

There was a fairly regular circuit of Sunday
afternoon singings in churches in and around
Amarillo. One of the prime factors involved in this
was the growing popularity of the gospel quartet.
The genius behind the gospel quartet movement was
V. O. Stamps, a deep bass from Dallas. He was in
the music publishing business, turning out paperback
songbooks and singing in a quartet named for him,
The Stamps Quartet. They traveled all around the
area, singing and attracting crowds and other groups
who were eager to appear with them.

Their expenses were borne in several ways, as I
recall. Instead of an admission fee, the audience
expressed its appreciation by making a small financial
contribution called a "love offering."

They also made considerable money from the sale
of their songbooks. Here, you could lay your hands
on the latest hits from the Stamps Publishing House.
Frequently, churches used the quartet books as their
only hymnals. These book sales were the
predecessors of the record sales most groups use
today to raise additional income.

Another phase of the Stamps Quartet music
business was a daily radio program, broadcast over

one of the powerful stations in Dallas. For most of my life, the most important time of the day (except for *the Lone Ranger* on Monday, Wednesday and Friday nights at 6:30 p.m.) was the fifteen minutes at lunchtime when the Stamps were singing! You even had to whisper, "Pass the salt." We listened as the quartet sang such hits as "Looking for a City," "Satisfied with Jesus in my Heart Today," and "The Jericho Road." The theme song for the broadcast was "Give the World a Smile Every Day." The Stamps Quartet *did* give our world a smile every day! Dad helped . . .

V. O. Stamps would begin the number with a low, slurring bass lead that required several seconds to bring the word "giiiiivvveeeee" up to the proper key. Dad always joined in with V. O. I thought he did an equally fine "giiiiivvveeeee." He was undiscovered radio quality!

Many of the songs my mother taught me came from these songbooks from traveling quartets. I stood on my metal folding chair Sunday afternoon after Sunday afternoon "Clinging to the Old Rugged Cross," hoping for a "Cabin in the Corner of Gloryland," and was utterly "Satisfied with Jesus in my Heart Today." Satisfied, that is, if I could figure out what "clinging" meant. At age five I had a hard time with "clinging . . ."

Perhaps it was destiny. Perhaps providence. Perhaps inevitable. One Sunday afternoon I sang on a program in Amarillo *with* the Stamps Quartet! V.O. was there and heard me sing. He was touched and moved; he sensed some talent here that ought to be developed and shared with unsuspecting but waiting America! He said so to my parents after we were dismissed from the afternoon singing. I never did get in on the particulars, but I do know that at age five I was on the train with my mother to Dallas to appear as a featured soloist on V. O. Stamps' famous *All Night Singing,* broadcast live on the radio from Dallas.

The *All Night Singing* was a broadcast that concluded the famous Stamps Singing School. This was a time of summer musical seminars and workshops for church musicians in the gospel music tradition. There were classes on playing the piano for accompaniment, for solo work, offertories, preludes, and quiet meditation. You could take classes in leading music for the congregation. You could get actual tips and pointers from the reigning masters of quartet music on the "how-to's" and "when-to's" and "where-to's" of your very own gospel quartet.

When the Singing School was over, there was the live broadcast of the *All Night Singing*—fantastic group singing from several thousand folks, numerous quartets and ensembles, featured soloists.

I was a featured soloist at age five.

I sang V.O. Stamps' very favorite song, "The Old Oaken Bucket." I took to the stage like a veteran. I climbed up into my folding metal chair in front of the tan-colored, flat-faced microphone. Mom hit the introduction. I sang my heart out. I looked straight ahead, hands at my sides, didn't let anything distract me. My pants stayed up. So did my joy and Mom's when it was over.

V. O. Stamps came out on stage to applaud with the audience. Tears were streaming down his cheeks. He put his arm around me and told the audience that I had just sung his favorite song so well that he would never sing it again. I felt very complimented!

He and my mom had a long talk when we were off stage. I learned later that he was so pleased with my singing that he wanted me to attend the Singing School the next summer. *As his guest*! He offered to let me stay in his home for the several-week duration of the school. He and his wife would "love to have me." I would attend the Singing School at no expense whatever. I would have to complete my first year of public school that coming year and be able to read well; then I could attend his school under those circumstances.

Mom was overcome with gratitude and appreciation. She talked about her conversation with V. O. for days and days. She, along with my dad, looked forward to the following summer when I would go study the best kind of music "up on the mountain where the secrets are hidden."

All year long, people listened to me sing in church gatherings all over the Texas plains with the awareness that the following summer I would stay in V.O. Stamps' home and attend the Singing School. They came up after I had sung to tell me that they had heard me sing "The Old Oaken Bucket" when I was actually on the radio! It was a heady and high time for our family.

V. O. Stamps died the next spring. I never got to attend the Singing School.

Our family continued to grow. My sister, Patsy, was born when I was seven; Ken was born when I was ten. As I reflect on the state of our family, it is fairly obvious that Mother had less and less time and energy to pour into my musical career. The daily lessons faded away; the regular Sunday singings around the territory diminished. I no longer had the busy life of the traveling musician. But my course was set in so many ways.

I plowed into public school music with gusto. I had teachers who worked hard to teach us how to sing on key, stay together, sing out loud. I was uninhibited in any musical group. I let it all go with force and volume. I was a step ahead of most of the kids. None of them had sung on major radio, so I boomed out with authority! Almost every teacher from the outset gave me solo parts and encouraged my great interest in music.

I volunteered for school plays, loved to read and give reports in class, always had my hand up when the teacher needed a response to a question. I loved school!

Did Doris Nutt *give* that ability to her son? Did she make me an "up-front" kind of person? Did she cause me to have this love and interest? She and I would both say no. What we both have believed over the years is that God gave me special gifts that she sensed quite early. She encouraged them and gave them a climate suited to their development. God gave me a melody; she helped me learn to give it away.

God gave me a melody. And a very special mom . . .

AWE IN THE FAMILY

My Uncle J. C. is like the "home on the range." You never hear a discouraging word.

In each of the other children in his family, my mom included, you see some characteristics of my granddad. In J. C., you see almost all of them at once. He has the simple quietness, the same love of family, the same sparkling and crackling wit. He developed premature "crow's feet" beside his eyes from chronic grinning. Rusty grinning . . .

Let me explain "rusty grinning."

In West Texas there is some ancient potion in the water. It may be that the water is so scarce out there that it will leave a permanent mark on anyone who dares confiscate even a cupful. At about age fourteen, the natives of the area get rusty, brown teeth. It comes on slowly, reaching a peak at about age thirty. It is not so common today because of the balancing of fluoride in the water and special techniques to combat the problem. J. C. got a full shot and half-a-load more of rusty teeth than the average Texan. If he should have them pulled and new dentures made, my firm conviction is that he'd try to talk the dentist into making the new ones rust-colored!

His face now has little low canyons of wrinkle here and there. His hair is beautifully gray like Grandma's.He loves to hunt. He has a story for every occasion and a comeback to disable any pretender to his throne of fun in the vicinity. He exudes warmth and thoughtfulness. He puts folks at ease easily. He knows the names of every relative on both sides of his family. He has raised four children who *know* he didn't hang the moon; but they are reasonably certain that he directed the project.

His wife is Melba, "the toast of the household." The only person known to outsmile J. C. She smiles a lot because he was a real catch in the forties and a rare find anytime. Melba is like my wife, Eleanor— she'd have to take lessons to make enemies!

When I want to feel the strong touch of the best of my difficult early years, I go to see J. C. and Melba.

They live in Lubbock, Texas, where he has been the general manager of the *Lubbock Avalanche-Journal,* the local newspaper, for several years. Around the paper office, he is called "Ricky." I see them too seldom but usually right on time. When I'm there, I'm closest to "where I come from."

Earlier, I gave you a sampler of my great admiration for J. C. From my earliest days he was my hero. I was in awe of him. He could drive a big truck when he was fourteen years old. And he did. And he made money doing it. And he didn't have a license! He'd flash a rusty grin, slam it in gear, aim it in the general direction, and let it happen. That kind of abandon was exciting and thrilling for a little nephew following him around, imitating every move he made.

I'd wear his shirts, clump around in his shoes,

fumble around through his desk drawer looking for gum, shoelaces, pocket knives, or anything he had used that I could play with. The only label necessary was that it had belonged to J. C.

Every time I plow a field of memory, the hidden treasure is always J. C. In the great spirit of my granddad, he was my encourager. He loved to see me coming! He'd play ball with me, let me ride in the car with him, buy me gum or other treats at the store across the street. I *bothered* him occasionally; he *brothered* me always.

J. C. is a consummate storyteller. You can always spot one, even though they are rare. They always love the story so much that they get wrapped up in it and laugh at it and stay tickled at it long after it's told. He gets happy all over more than anywhere else when he starts in on a great story. It's into the well of his spirit I most frequently dip my bucket . . .

I can remember, even as a child, hanging on every story he told—about school, dates, church, work. I believed he could outrun, outjump, outthink, outdrive, outfight any living soul. And I really did want to be like him. So, I tried.

World War II erupted in my second-grade year. I don't remember much about its beginning; I was only seven years old. The nation was still reeling from the Depression; the war could not have come at a worse time.

The fathers of many boys my age were drafted for military service. Many of those men were killed in active duty. I was more fortunate than some of my friends. My dad was not drafted because of medical reasons. I breathed easier when he came back from the examination to report he'd been rejected.

Not so with J. C. He was taken into the Navy and served for a while. I do not know for certain how long he was in active service, but I do know that my granddad had died by this time, and his death, along with J. C.'s absence, really took the joy from Grandma's life. I shared her grief and worried and cried and watched for mail right along with her.

But J. C. was discharged in fine shape and returned home with hope and a new sense of direction. When he announced his news to the family, the whole clan rejoiced. He had made a decision to become a Methodist minister. He would be entering college to study for the ministry the very next term.

At this particular time, our family was not involved in church at all. My dad had left the dairy and gone into business on his own as a dry cleaner. He worked hard and long hours, usually seven days each week. I'm not sure that the job was the only reason we were not in church, but it was one reason.

Even though we were not active church-goers, J. C.'s intention to enter the ministry was a cause of pride and celebration. I can remember the way I announced it to my friends: "My Uncle J. C. is going to be a minister!"

About that time I was in Mrs. Sorrenti's fifth-grade class at Alice Landergin Elementary School. One day she was asking each of the pupils in our room about hunches and dreams of vocation and lifework. I heard the typical answers: fireman, nurse, cowboy, doctor, teacher. Then she asked me what I wanted to be when I grew up. If I were asked that question today, I'd say, *"Mature." Then,* though, I said, "A minister."

She'd probably never even heard a *minister's* child say that! The class turned with her and looked at me in some hybrid combination of surprise and disbelief.

I was beaming in the knowledge that I was going to do what J. C. was going to do. I didn't even go to church, was not even singing on folding chairs on Sunday afternoons anymore; still, I was going to be a minister. Second choices might be railroad engineer or mountain lion hunter; but for today, my decision was firm: I was going to be a minister!

The attention of the class made me a bit uncomfortable, but I held steady. A few snickers. A couple of chuckles. Two pointed fingers. Then Mrs. Sorrenti broke the silence.

"That's just beautiful, Grady." The class looked at her and then at me again. This time they smiled, too. It was the following summer that I was to meet Roy B. Flippo, and the ministry was to have a "forever face." I would know it up close, first hand, face to face. I would have a genuine model and a Moses to follow up the mountain.

For now, I had J. C. as a hero and the approval of my teacher and the smiles of my classmates. And she was right! It was beautiful . . .

The year *my* teeth were about to rust, we moved from Amarillo to Jacksonville, Texas. For the first time in my life I was going to be removed from my close ties with Grandma and J. C. I regretted that more than any part of the move. But love is not measured in miles . . .

J. C. has been in Lubbock, Texas, now for many years. I get to see him frequently on trips into the city and the area. With him I still feel the warmth of my childhood as strongly as I can smell the Cashmere Bouquet and lavender soap in Grandma's bathroom. He redirected his life shortly after beginning college and did not make the ministry his vocation. However, he has been an active layman and lay minister in the Methodist church and gives enormous energy and loyalty to his church.

Our visits are fun. I love to walk in on him without letting him know I am in town. He looks up with an expression that says: "Lay it on the desk, thank you. . ." Then he'll grin rust at me and give me a big hug and start introducing me—six feet, four inches tall—around the offices as his "little nephew." We all have a good laugh, then I hit him up for a bed for the night and free lunch. He loves it.

Sometimes he catches me off guard. Once I was walking through the giant air terminal in Dallas-Fort Worth about 8:00 in the morning. I was tired from getting up early and from having stayed up late—a lethal combination! In the hustle/bustle/jostle of the travelers, I heard my name, slow-drawled, West Texas style: "Graaaady Nuuuuutt . . ." I glanced around, trying to look professionally happy after an amateur use of late night. It was J. C. leaning against a wall in a fine-looking suit and new boots. I started laughing and walked over to him. He acted like he'd left me only the moment before to get a cup of coffee and had just walked back in the room. He flashed some rust at me and told me he was waiting for a good-looking woman who was going to join him for a trip to the Bahamas. I pressed him a bit: "Come on, what are you really doing here?" He nodded behind me. I turned to look. Out of the ladies' restroom came a good-looking woman. It was Melba, his wife. We all had a super laugh. They were on their way to celebrate their thirtieth wedding anniversary.

All day I celebrated the brief touch with my hero.

I have a good friend named Cotton Ivy. Cotton is a marvelous storyteller from West Tennessee. On one of his albums he tells a story about getting new shoes. He tried to make them last as long as possible, so he didn't really wear them until cold

weather arrived, past frost, full into snow.
Barefooted on a cold, frosty morning, he'd go down
to the barn to get the cows up for milking. He says
that when he'd find a cow "layin' down," he'd get
her up and then run to stand in the warm spot
where she'd been!

I stand frequently in the warm spots that J. C. has
created in my life.

The warmest of all happened a few years back. I
had driven a rental car from Abilene, Texas, to
Tahoka, Texas, (near Lubbock) to speak for a
meeting of the Chamber of Commerce. I invited
J. C. and Melba to drive down the thirty miles or so
to be my guests. They came. After the banquet I
followed them back to Lubbock and spent the night.

The next morning I was to fly out of Lubbock at
6:30. That meant getting up at 4:45, leaving the
house no later than 5:30 to get my car and baggage
checked in at the terminal. I began to tell them both
good-bye and *thank-you* as we prepared for bed.
J. C. said that he'd just tell me *good-bye* when I got
ready to leave the next morning. I assured him there
was no reason to get up so early, that I could get up
quietly and drive out without disturbing them. He
insisted that he wanted to get up and see me off.

At 5:00 a.m., a coffee mug in each hand, he
came back to my bedroom to give me a "shot of
wake-up" before I hit the road. He sat on the bed in
his robe and slippers as I got dressed for the day and
repacked. About 5:25 I hauled my baggage out to
the car, started it up, got the heater working for a
few minutes, and came back in to thank him for the
good visit. We stood by the back door, a little uncle,
a big nephew—both big to each other.

"Enjoyed having you with us again," he said. I
assured him it was mutual. "And," he continued, "it

was really good to hear you do your stuff last night."
I "allowed as how" it had been very special to me to
have them at the dinner. I tried hard to be myself as
I entertained, even with my hero in the room. Then,
like Roy Flippo put a face on ministry for me, J. C.
put the "forever face" on affirmation . . .

"You're really good. I thought you were just really
good. I'm sorry it took so long for me to get to hear
you, but I am so glad we got to hear you. And I
knew you'd be good." And slowly the grin started to
rust. "I just didn't think you'd be *that* good!"

I couldn't hug God, so I hugged J. C. I couldn't
talk. I was afraid my face would break if I made a
move of any kind. I hugged him a long time. Then I
went out on that frosty morning and got into my car
with the heater running. It would have been a warm
spot even if I hadn't started the engine yet!

And I drove to the airport.

Crying . . .

CALLING PARSON TO PERSON

Any discussion of pivotal characters in my life has to include Roy B. Flippo. You pronounce that: *FLIP-o*.

I mention Roy occasionally when I am speaking to groups, and his name always gets a good chuckle. It is a bit unusual. I usually pause for a moment when this happens—to point out that no person with a normal name has ever blessed my life!

And no one in my childhood and early teens ever blessed my life more than Roy B. Flippo!

Roy was a friend of my parents before I ever knew him. As far as I can remember, my first encounter with him was a "counter-encounter" in my father's dry cleaning establishment in Amarillo, Texas. Roy brought suits into the cleaners on Monday or Tuesday, still sweaty and damp from a hard Sunday of "real preaching!"

Roy had the voice of a non-stop auctioneer, the physical involvement and exertion of a "by-the-weed cotton chopper!" He had the no-nonsense commitment of a thrice-stoned-and-left-for-dead apostle, the certainty of a sky diver, and the zeal of a

non-smoker! In short, he took faith and scriptures
and preaching and sinners seriously. *Very*
seriously . . .

At the counter at my dad's cleaners that day, Roy
invited me to come to Vacation Bible the next week.
At that time I was not attending church anywhere.
Dad was trying to support four children and his only
wife with the sweat of his brow seven days per week.
When I was not in school, I was at the cleaning plant
working. I swept floors, helped out in the cleaning
room, waited on the customers at the front counter,
played pranks and tricks on the employees, and
operated a small bicycle-repair shop in the back alley
of the place.

I did not like labor then; I like it no better now. I
definitely was interested in Vacation Bible School! I'd
have gone to a dog fight as a *participant* to get away
from the shop for a week!

Vacation Bible School was meant for kids like me!
I loved it all—all except the Kool-Aid! It was never
iced and always orange. That, with ginger snaps,
and your smile was never the same again . . .

We sang songs. Like "Deep and Wide" (with
motions); like "Rolled Away, Rolled Away." It gave
me the "Joy, Joy, Joy, Joy Down in My Heart" and
"if the devil didn't like it he could sit on a tack"!
(That may have been my favorite part!)

I heard Bible stories. Old stories. For-the-first-
time-in-my-life stories. I learned about Jonah, Noah,
David, Goliath, Zacchaeus, Paul/Saul. I couldn't get
enough! I was like a sweets addict at the Hershey
factory! I brought my Bible every day, learned how
to find the verses, memorized the verses, and felt as
much at home as a Norwegian on skis.

Roy always showed special interest in me during
all these very special days in my life. He knew my

name. He called on me during story-time. He asked
me to sing a verse alone once; he said "Amen"
when I finished. He rubbed my head several times.
He didn't mind that I stayed close to him and drank
from his attentiveness 'til city bus time.

It was hard not to feel special . . .

I worked hard at Vacation Bible School. It was
almost not *vacation* to me! I learned my memory
verse every day. I went back to the cleaners and
sneaked time away from my chores to hide back in
the big boxes of wire coat hangers and read again
and again the Bible story of the day.

I was a marvelous group participant. I loved to
carry the flag. By the second morning I knew the
pledge to the Christian flag perfectly. I did all the
motions to the songs with flagrant gusto. I always
had a nickel for the offering. I *never* missed on a "Sit
Down" or "Stand Up" chord!

Commencement approached; it was Friday night.
Roy asked me to take a major part. He wanted me
to tell one of the flannelgraph stories. It was to be
my first "public speaking" appearance; I was
honored and delighted. I was also curious about how
the flannelgraph worked. It was amazingly
simple . . .

A board, plywood usually, was covered with
flannel. The board was about three feet wide and
two feet high. It rested on its side on a wooden,
rickety easel. In individual classes—when you were
not up in front of the entire group in the sanctuary—
it was frequently placed on the music-holding lip of
an upright piano.

Pictures of biblical characters and scenes were cut
out, rather like paper dolls, with a flannel backing
glued on. Then, as you told the story of David and
Goliath, for instance, you could put the picture on

the flannelgraph board and it would just stay there!
I was given a very special story to tell. I got the box
with the fuzzy-backed characters. For two afternoons
and most of one evening, I practiced placing the
characters on my bedspread. On Friday night I got
up a bit nervously to tell the parents and my fellow
Vacation Bible Schoolmates the story of the Hebrew
children in the fiery furnace: Shadrach, Meshach,
and Abednego. Folks laughed several times through
my presentation. You usually didn't hear laughter
during Bible stories. I rather liked it . . .

After the commencement exercises I learned why
they were laughing. All night I had pronounced
Abednego wrong! I said—every time—*Ab-ah-NING-go!*

I loved being in this church. I loved Roy Flippo. I
loved Bible stories. I loved "Deep and Wide" and
hoped even the Devil would get the "Joy, Joy, Joy,
Joy Down in His Heart"! The soil of my life was
broken by the plowpoint of Roy's concern.

That week was the beginning of one of the most
exciting and growth-filled years of my entire life.
Amarillo, Texas, at that time was a city of about
55,000 people. Our home was on the south side of
the city, almost on the city limits. The Bethel
Missionary Baptist Church was on the north side of
the city, almost on the city limits. I rode the bus
across the city on Sunday mornings, Sunday
evenings, Wednesday evenings for church services. I
paid my own bus fare out of my odd jobs and
occasional tips collected at the cleaners.

I hung on every word and move of Roy B. Flippo.
He had a black Shaeffer pen and pencil set, pre-ball
point days, that he wore in his outside coat pocket. I
always had at least two pencils in my shirt pocket,
one a Scripto fat-lead type. I wanted to be like him
in every way.

I followed along in my Bible in every sermon, Bible study, devotional. I underlined the verses, circled the verses, tried to memorize the verses, wrote down the locations of the crucial ones in the inside cover of my own Bible. I started running out of margin space in my copy, thought many times that I wish Scofield hadn't written so much at the bottom of the page. Maybe Roy would come out with a version of his own and we could refer to the Flippo Notes at the bottom of the page . . .

I started a church of my own in my garage. I held my Bible like Roy, pointed like Roy, frowned like Roy, rubbed the heads of children like Roy. I preached fiery sermons on imminent issues like the Battle of Armageddon, the symbolism in Daniel, dancing, writing on or even reading the school bathroom walls. Sermons intended to redirect life. Sermons full of power and conviction. Sermons to strike repentance into the hearts of each and every hearer in my hot, summer garage! I was dealing with the downfallen, the liars, the thieves, the cheaters, the selfish, and the Godforsaken.

And the fifth and sixth grades at Alice Landergin Elementary were full of them!

A year of that kind of faithfulness and development brought me to a crucial decision. It occurred after my hero gave me one of the rare chances that comes to a potential leader . . .

I was twelve. It was early May. I had been counted among the faithful for almost a year now. Roy called me aside after Sunday School one Sunday to ask for my help.

"I'd like for you to be one of the leaders in Vacation Bible School this summer."

"Me? A leader? In Bible School?" I could hardly grasp the whole truth, and "nothin' but the truth"!

"Yes. You've been faithful. You've grown. You've been writing in your margins. I think you've come to a place where you can be a big help to us," he said.

"How?" I wondered out loud. "What could I do to help?"

"I'd like for you to be one of the workers with the primary and beginner children. You could do flannelgraph stories . . ."

(I definitely lit up!)

". . . and lead songs with motions. We could use you all week, if you're interested . . ."

IF I were interested! I responded like a low flame getting oxygen! "I'd love it! Oh, Brother Roy, thank you! I can hardly believe it! A *leader* in Bible School . . .!"

To go any higher I'd have to come down and start over!

It was one of the most enjoyable weeks of my life. I was a *leader*. My opinion mattered. Kids were looking up to me. Every five-and six-year-old child had two pencils in his shirt pocket!

I got to do another story for commencement, sang a solo, knew my way around even the adults, felt comfortable, belonged. My folks came for commencement, beaming profusely. I had made the family look just fine.

Then Roy sprang another surprise.

He asked my parents to let me accompany him on three revival meetings he was to preach that summer. I would do flannelgraph stories and lead songs with motions each evening for the younger children right before the evening revival service began. The parents would be in prayer meetings while this was going on. I was elated! My folks approved the idea. I was going on the road with Roy B. Flippo as probably the first child flannelgraph evangelist in the world!

Those three revival meetings gave permanent direction to my life. Looking back from the vantage point of many changes and decisions, I still maintain that those three trips with Roy are the foundation upon which most of my faith has been built.

In the first meeting I came to grips with the need to commit my life to Jesus Christ as a disciple and follower. My language has always been the language of my church—this was my faithful *profession of faith*.

In the second meeting I realized that I needed to make that decision known to my church, the Bethel Missionary Baptist Church in Amarillo, Texas. So, we came home from the revival and Roy promptly baptized me by immersion. I was "dead to my old way of life; I was raised to walk in newness of life"! By agreeing to baptize me, the church agreed to be strength for my journey!

In the third meeting I felt compelled to "surrender my life to the ministry." I felt many compatible emotions: a minister's example of concern and friendship; a joy at being able to share in worship and teaching; a love for music and preaching; a desire to know more and share all I came to know; a love for people; a desire to help.

As I have matured and considered the decision I made to become a minister, I am certain that it was the right thing for me to do. I have seen my life take many unexpected turns, though, and I have wound up with a different understanding of *ministry* than that of being a pastor.

Roy helped me sense a vital factor in Christian growth and decision-making: God will not lead or call us to do or perform a task we are not capable of handling. God will not give us strengths and gifts that cannot be used by Him. I will find his direction for my life in the area of the things I am able to do!

Roy sensed my gifts and showed them to me. Roy was a beautiful example of sensitivity and concern. Roy has been a model for me, a friend to me, another father to me.

And you can write that down with either pencil in your pocket!

PRUNING WITH A
NEW WRINKLE

Roy Flippo planted the "tree of my faith." Hoyt Mulkey pruned and groomed it!

Hoyt Mulkey is probably the reason I laugh like I do. Every now and then someone who hears me speak asks, "Where did you get that funny laugh?" I almost always reply, "From Hoyt Mulkey."

He and I are both natives of Amarillo, Texas. He is seven years older than I. My parents knew his parents. I attended junior high school with two of his brothers, Charles and Rex. I didn't meet Hoyt until after I moved to Jacksonville, Texas, when I was a junior in high school.

Hoyt came to Jacksonville as a part of a youth evangelism team. He led the music and sang like no one I had ever heard. Until he got there, I had the best voice in Jacksonville! It was a hard pill to swallow that there was another great voice out there! At first I was resentful, competitive. Then I became fascinated and friendly. It was one of the great thrills of my life to be asked to sing a duet with him one night!

We met sometime during the summer. After

53

school started the next fall, I got a marvelous surprise. Hoyt came back—on weekends only—as the minister of music at the Central Baptist Church in Jacksonville! He was there the last two years of my high school days.

Hoyt was still in seminary in Fort Worth, Texas, at the time. However, he moved to Jacksonville eventually and rented a house right across the street from the high school. It made visiting with him simple—I could catch him on his way to work each day. The church was only three blocks from his home, so I could walk over there after school and give him the benefit of my presence, insights, and ukulele-playing progress!

Hoyt had inspired me to learn to play the ukulele. He had been in Hawaii during World War II and knew a pile of Hawaiian music. He could accompany most of it on a ukulele. I learned almost all of his repertoire, and I sounded just like him— nearly . . .

He was a special friend to me. I didn't have many nice clothes, so he let me borrow shoes, slacks, jackets, shirts on special occasions when I wanted to impress a date or needed to look right in front of an audience. My very favorite shoes in the whole world were his blue simulated-alligator, wing-tipped, suede-inset, steel-tapped "dress shoes"! You could hear me coming on carpet! They were two sizes too small for me, but they looked so good I just celebrated the pain!

Hoyt was funny. He told crazy jokes and got tickled at the punch lines himself. He did some pantomimes. He loved to barbershop-quartet sing. He got one started with two of my best friends and me. We really learned a lot from him, sang in and around the area a great deal, and loved every minute of it. He gave me a sense of comfort in front of an audience. It never mattered to him whether we were at a Rotary luncheon or in a church service— he knew how to do the right kind of music for any group, and he loved singing for all of them.

I was not a member of his church. I just attended so much everyone *thought* I was a member! You may not be aware of the multitudes and varieties of Baptists, but there are many different kinds of Baptists—as *different* as the colors of M & M's candy coating *outside*, as *alike* as the chocolate *inside*!

My parents had become quite active in Roy Flippo's church after I made my decision to become a minister. In fact, eighteen months later, my father became a minister! He left his business in Amarillo and moved our family to Jacksonville, Texas, so he could attend a small Baptist college located there and supported by Missionary Baptist churches. Hoyt was at the Central Baptist Church, a member church of the Southern Baptist Convention. My folks were rather uptight about my involvement in Hoyt's church, but they did allow me to attend there in order to sing with him and be around him.

It has always pleased me that Hoyt never mentioned my joining his church. He used me every Sunday night, I believe, for the two years he was minister of music there. I sang solos, duets, quartet numbers, and led the music when he was away on vacation. He was interested in giving me an opportunity to grow in my faith and to share my talents and gifts. He handled that aspect of our relationship perfectly, and I am grateful!

Hoyt had attended Wayland Baptist College in Plainview, Texas. In his senior year he was the first president of the Wayland International Choir under the direction of Shelby Collier. The choir had been

Shelby's dream for some time because the student body had a remarkable number of foreign students. He wanted the choir to learn the music of many nations and to wear costumes from these lands in their concerts. It may have been the most unique college choir ever assembled!

In the spring of my junior year in high school, the Wayland International Choir came, at Hoyt's invitation, to sing in the Central Baptist Church of Jacksonville, Texas.

It turned out to be one of the highlights of my life. I heard the finest choir I had ever heard! I saw costumes and students from Korea, China, Greece, Mexico, Hawaii, South America, Japan and others. I stared and listened in "slack-jawed amazement," to quote my friend, Pete Hester . . .

Hoyt got me an audition with Shelby. Shelby liked my voice. On the basis of the audition and Hoyt's recommendation, I was given a scholarship to Wayland along with my best friend in Jacksonville, Elmore Averyt. I was going to the school where Hoyt had gone, to study with Hoyt's teacher, and to sing in Hoyt's choir so I could graduate, buy some blue suede wing-tips, and be just like Hoyt!

And you wonder why I laugh funny!

The saddest night I ever experienced before going to college was the night Hoyt left Jacksonville. The week before Elmore and I graduated from high school, he moved to another church nearer the seminary. We drove around in Hoyt's 1949 Studebaker, in second gear for over ten miles, just remembering and laughing and talking and singing . . .

. . . and trying not to cry.

But I did.

Our paths have crossed and intertwined and mingled through the years. It was through knowing

him that I met my wife, Eleanor. He later became
the minister of music at her home church in
Memphis, Tennessee. In fact, he assumed his new
duties at the church on Sunday morning, June 16,
1957. Eleanor and I were married on Tuesday night,
June 18, 1957, and Hoyt sang for our wedding!

Hoyt only served one church where I did not assist
him in some special way during his stay on the staff.
I led music for revivals, spoke for retreats,
entertained for banquets, was camp pastor for music
camps. He always used me for the various gifts he
saw in me, which he had encouraged in me. I had in
him the remarkable combination of mentor and
brother, teacher and friend, encourager and
corrector. My hunch is that most of the shape of my
personality is cast in his mold.

Until I was twenty-five years old, no single person
had a more significant impact on how I looked at
life, at my gifts, at my role in ministry, than Hoyt
Mulkey. It reminds me of my first month on the
campus at Wayland College . . .

Some of the students who were seniors when I
arrived had been freshmen when Hoyt was president
of the International Choir. One of them was assistant
accompanist of the choir, Ledale Meeks. She was
sitting on a table top in the main foyer of the
administration building one afternoon as I walked
past. I had been teased a bit by a few of the older
students about "singing like Hoyt, laughing like Hoyt,
entertaining like Hoyt." Ledale watched me walk by
and commented to another student standing close
by: "He even *walks* like him!" She didn't even have
to say, like whom? I knew. Like Hoyt Mulkey!

I blushed for a moment, partly out of pride, partly
out of self-consciousness. Then, I grinned at Ledale
and walked on . . .

. . . like Hoyt!

EIGHT MILES FROM THE NEAREST KNOWN SIN

Where is Wayland Baptist College? Eight miles from the nearest known sin!

That's practically true. The college is located in Plainview, Texas. An appropriately named town. Looking *at* it or looking *out of* it—*plain view*!

Plainview is in the "panhandle" of Texas, the square top of Texas. Up near the north pole in winter. Down near the equator in summer.

West Texas is the world headquarters of *nothing*. There is probably more *nothing* in West Texas than anywhere else in the world. And the folks out there love their *nothing*. They are devoted to and protective of their *nothing*. Each year they build new barbed-wire fences around their *nothing*. They are determined to keep your *something* off their *nothing*!

It was an ideal place for a Baptist college. Parents could send a child two hundred miles away to school, then stand on the porch and watch *every move he or she made*!

Great memories! I enjoyed every aspect of campus life—except the studies. I have gleaned more stories from that single year than from any other period in my life. It was there that John Gatlin inspired me to learn to play the piano by ear. It was there that I almost scared Ed Clark to death in the city cemetery one night! It was there I was wrapped head-to-toe in athletic tape one autumn night and left for an hour in the cold grass on the colder ground—a mummy itching to get loose! It was there I broke my ties with home and learned to make it on my own. It was there I started getting such good help for the journey . . .

It was an ideal campus for me. Small, close-knit, unpretentious, conservative in most respects, progressive in a few. The most progressive dimension of the college life was its international make-up. There were about 500 students enrolled during my year there. The amazing thing was the fact that there were twenty-two (count 'em!) nations represented in the student body!

The genius behind that feat was Dr. Bill Marshall. He was president of Wayland for several years. My freshman year was his last year; it had nothing to do with my being there! He had a beautiful and practical theory/vision about mission work: Bring outstanding Christian young people from other nations to our school; give them a solid Christian-college education, and send them back among their native peoples with a desire to share their faith. They would readily fit into their own cultures and traditions; they would speak the language; they would be able to eat the food!

Wayland was truly the international campus. I lived in a suite with seven other students—two per room. I lived with a student from Hawaii. Hawaii was not yet a state, so he qualified as a "foreigner." He also looked like one. Across the hall from me were two black students from South America. Until they opened their mouths, you thought they were just U.S.A. blacks. When they talked you knew they weren't from around here. Next door to me was a student from Mexico rooming with a student from China. Snack time was wild in their room—Oriental teas and jalapeno peppers! Next to them and the bathroom at the end of the hall were two ordinary United-States types.

I even showered and shaved international!

I went to Wayland because Hoyt Mulkey had sold me on the International Choir. Very quickly I found that I belonged there for all the right reasons. A crucial reason was the healthy and purely Christian attitude I encountered in this atmosphere regarding the touchy area of race relationships.

Before Selma and Montgomery and lunch counters and back-of-the-bus boycotts and Martin Luther King, Jr., I saw young people face their prejudice and their superstition and their suspicion and become friends. One of my proudest days as a student came when our class went up to a state park nearby for an outing. Picnicking and swimming all day! No classes!

We were met at the entrance to the pool and told by the officials that we could not bring the black students in with us. This was in the spring of 1953. The attitude was common in this part of the country. But we were so accustomed to being with our black student friends that we were stunned and shocked by the rule. We argued and pled with the gatekeeper. We were firmly refused entrance if the black students came with us. The class called a huddle.

In our discussion we determined to return to the campus and have our picnic on the lawn behind the administration building. With quiet conviction we went back to school with the unanimous feeling that we were doing the right thing. We'd rather give up a swim than a conviction!

One interesting hurdle that was cleared had to do with the black students who wanted to enter from Plainview and the surrounding United States. Dr. Marshall pressed the trustees to establish a policy that said students from the homeland were just as welcome as the students from Nigeria with large, wide scars on their cheeks. He was upheld by courageous folks who were determined to be fair in their dealings. And to be Christian.

It was from this policy of accepting students from all over the world that the International Choir got its name. Students secured costumes for us from their homelands. Then, they taught us their music phonetically. It was possible for a student with an Amarillo-nasality to sing Japanese and Latvian! He might not know what he meant, but he was not terribly concerned. He also took algebra . . .

We sang for churches and schools, civic clubs, and group meetings of all kinds. We traveled widely and were quite well known. The choir was the primary public relations arm for the school. We made four major tours each year, usually in the territories from which we drew most of our students. We would appear on stage—forty-two strong—costumed in the fashions of many lands and nations, directed by a polished and seasoned showman, Shelby Collier, wearing a Mexican formal suit. It was festive and celebrative and memorable.

We had fun in the choir. On the road. In rehearsals. In concert! I especially enjoyed myself in concerts. Mostly because I didn't do a very good job of learning the foreign languages. I bluffed a lot, acted like I knew what was going on. The rest of the time I just faked it!

One Russian song was my favorite. It sounded like this in Russian phonics: "GO DEE PROSH LEE DAV NO, STRASS TEE O TEE LEE . . ." I'd sing with Russian gusto until we came to that line. Then I'd sing the last phrase: "FROSTY OLD TEA LEAVES!" I had another favorite phrase in the same song: "MAY NAY ZA BEE TAY, DAV NO *OOOJ*, USH LA!" The "*oooj*" was to sound strained and heavy, like rowing with the Volga boatmen. I'd sing the phrase *my* way: "MAYONNAISE ON A BEET CAKE." I could even get the music *majors* tickled!

We'd use the new languages to our advantage when we traveled. In a restaurant, I would look as "foreign" as possible and stare in confused amazement at the American menu. The waitress would wait, pencil poised over the little green pad. I'd look at my cohort and quote a line from a Finnish anthem. He'd look at the waiting waitress and say: "He'd like a cheeseburger, mayonnaise instead of mustard, French fries, and a Dr. Pepper . . ." I'd interrupt him with another phrase from the anthem. He'd continue: ". . . with no onion." She'd be overly gracious and accommodating. After all, she had a real foreign person right at her table in Roswell, New Mexico! She'd hustle around and work hard and smile at me a lot. I'd nod and look like I was from some wooden-shoe country. And I could really look non-American.

As we left I'd confuse her beyond words with a good old "Thank you very much"—spoken in perfect Amarillo!

Speaking of Amarillo, we had a classic episode there one afternoon at the Amarillo Air Force Base. The base authority in the public relations sector had arranged for us to sing in full costume for the international pilot trainees on the base. They were

from many of the Allied countries in Western
Europe. Shelby was ecstatic! A chance to sing for
many nations in the languages of many nations! We
did our full international concert and brought down
the house.

After the concert was over, the cadets mobbed us
to thank us and to see the lovely American girls up
close. One native of Finland sought a moment of
privacy with Shelby. Shelby came back from the brief
encounter with stun and shock on his face. Also a
trace of embarrassed.

The young man had told Shelby that one of the
songs we sang as a "Latvian hymn" was in fact not a
hymn at all! It was—and I quote!—"One of the
dirtiest little alley songs in our country!" Latvia was
dead, but not the dirty little alley song!

However, we continued using it all year because it
was already in our printed program!

The primary "shaping" of my life at this time was
done by Shelby Collier. He was a marvelous man.
He and his wife had no children of their own, so he
adopted the choir. He saw each of us as "one of his
own." I discovered that fact when I got off the train
with a flat-top haircut, burr-waxed until it looked like
a brush on its back! He took one look at me and
marched me off to his barber on the ground floor of
Plainview's largest hotel. He instructed the barber
that I was one of his boys, and from that day on I
was to have my hair grown out and cut as he
instructed! No monkey business! It didn't take too
many weeks until I had a beautiful, dishwater-
blonde, Vitalis-laden set of ducktails! Elvis with a
bleach job!

As my hair grew, I grew. Some of it was painful,
much of it was pure pleasure. It was the beginning of
the carefree fifties . . . the war was over; the jobs

were plentiful; the folks were getting caught up on savings accounts, and Fleers Bubble Gum was back doing combat with Bazooka! I thought I had found a slice of paradise. I never wanted to leave my new home at Wayland, my comfortable relationship with Shelby, the dirty little alley song . . .

. . . but, I couldn't type.

Let me explain that. I had taken typing in high school and was passed by a generous teacher who gave me some credit for being business manager of the school paper. After an entire year of typing, I could only type *nine* words per minute. Before counting off for errors! In the spring of my freshman year at Wayland, I took beginning typing again. After a semester of conscientious effort, I improved my score to *twelve* words per minute! And they got tired of counting my errors!

There was a rule at Wayland regarding scholarships. You could not retain a scholarship if you made even one failing grade on your final scores. You were required to forfeit the scholarship help for one semester and pass all your work. Only then could you be reinstated to the normal scholarship agreement.

I had a half-scholarship in the choir. I failed typing in the spring of my freshman year and lost all of my half-scholarship! Shelby called me a week before registration for the fall term to tell me the bad news. I was crushed! I thought it was a Latvian plot! I hung up the phone and cried.

Without the scholarship I couldn't attend Wayland. I was running several directions all at once trying to earn even the additional half of my school expenses plus spending money. I was pressing pants for a dry cleaner, serving in the dining hall, mopping in the dorm, and singing in a quartet several nights per month. I really had no choice. I had to drop out of Wayland. I *felt* like a crop failure must *look*.

I decided to spend that semester at a junior college in Jacksonville, live with my folks, find some part-time work, and pass every class. I would not take typing! It had already caused a major backspace in my life! With good grades in hand, I'd return to Wayland and resume my role in the choir as a skinny Russian Cossack!

I could not know then that I'd never be back as a student. However, I shall always cherish the warmth and encouragement of Shelby Collier, the experiences with a "living color" student body, the friends that have lasted for this much of a lifetime, and a feeling of belonging as solid as a cattleman's handshake!

It may not have been heaven on earth, but for me it was within eight miles of it . . .

ACADEMIA NUTT

I couldn't afford to go to Wayland for my sophomore year; I couldn't afford *not* to go to Baylor when the chance came.

The chance came, typically for me, untypically. I was back in my hometown, Jacksonville, Texas, attending two junior colleges simultaneously. Don't re-read that. I did say *two*.

Even though it's a small town, Jacksonville has two colleges: Jacksonville Baptist College (named for the town and the one true religion!) and Lon Morris College. It's Methodist and, therefore, highly suspect. They baptize wrong and then build a college to argue for it . . . *puzzling!*

Jacksonville Baptist College, or JBC as it was shorthanded in the vernacular, was supported by my folks' church—the Missionary Baptists. Lon Morris was never a consideration in my college-considering days because they just might teach other things as strangely as how to baptize wrong! I would never have considered it if Zula Pearson had not recruited me for a melodrama.

I had been quite serious about drama in high

school. Our drama coach, Mr. James Everett, was a superb director. He was also one of the finest English teachers ever to conjugate a preposition! He got me into several plays during my senior year in high school. One was a one-act play that we entered in the state One-Act Play Competition. The title of the play was "The Undercurrent." I was the male lead. This competition had several levels where you risked elimination *en route* to the finals. We survived every contest and won the state finals. The best in the entire state! We were beside ourselves with basic delirium!

I was named Best Actor in two of the preliminary meets, was named to the All-Star cast in a third, and was named Best Actor in the final competition. I had an entire page devoted to me in the annual that year. It was the highlight of my entire school career.

Zula Pearson was the drama coach at Lon Morris, an outstanding individual with skills in her field that belonged in some of the finer theaters in the country. She obviously knew a great deal more about drama than she did about baptism! How they ever kept her in a small Texas town I'll never know. You will surely know one of her most famous student actors: Sandy Duncan, television performer and magna-cum-talent.

Zula had seen me perform in high school. When she learned that I was back in town for at least a semester, she called me to talk about a special project she was spearheading. She asked me to consider working on it with her.

It was a classic idea. She wanted to revive the old *J. Doug Morgan Tent Show.* This was a traveling road show that moved around the country at the turn of the century in horse-drawn wagons—circus style. They would set up tents, then perform on makeshift stages. Their repertoire consisted of individual stage acts (similar to vaudeville) and the exaggerated "Boo-the-Villain" melodramas. The company wintered in Jacksonville.

J. Doug Morgan's widow still lived on the farm. It had been used for wintering the horses that pulled the wagons and for storage of the costumes and stage equipment in a large barn. Zula wanted to get Mrs. Morgan to allow us to do some of J. Doug's old melodramas as a community theater project. We would erect a large tent on a vacant lot near the college, set up our stage and lighting, and produce a fun time for the whole town. Mrs. Morgan had joyfully consented. Zula wanted it to be an annual event.

Zula had selected the first play: "Pure as the Driven Snow." She wanted me to play the lead role as *Leander Longfellow.* I would seek to save and marry Purity Dean, victim of the wiles of the merciless, saw-blade-wielding villain. For several years the tent show was a sell-out event with standing room only.

It didn't take long to get firmly entrenched again in the community life. I was attending JBC three mornings per week, driving a delivery car for a local dry cleaner, practicing for the melodrama nightly, dating occasionally but not regularly, and doing a bit of church work on the side. The tent show ended. Zula called me in for another conference. I drove the delivery car by, parked in a "Visitors" slot out in front of the administration building, and went to her office.

She had a new scheme. This time she wanted me to enroll at Lon Morris so I could play a lead role in a play she was going to produce for a national Methodist collegiate conference later in the winter.

Up in Kansas. Working with her excited me. I thought I could handle the inferior theology of the baptism department. And I had never been to Kansas. I enrolled at mid-term.

The play was a colossal success. We used eighteen actors to play fifty-four parts. I had four parts myself. The audience numbered almost 4,000. We did Christopher Frye's "Boy With A Cart." Tough work, but I loved it!

As we were putting the finishing touches on that play, she approached me with a new idea. Would I help her write a one-act play for the state Junior College One-Act Play Competition later in the spring? Would I! I played the lead role. I was named to the All-Star Cast. The play took first honors. Drama felt as comfortable as faded jeans . . .

Zula called again in the spring. Another proposal. I listened up . . .

She wanted me to drive over to Waco, Texas, with her the next week to visit Baylor University. Specifically, she wanted me to meet Paul Baker. He was an absolute genius in the theater. He was directing a new play by Gene McKinney, one of his colleagues. Zula wanted me to see the play, meet Baker, and consider trying for a scholarship in drama for the next fall. A scholarship to Baylor! And they knew about baptism! They taught it right!

So I visited Baylor with Zula. It is located on the Brazos River in Central Texas. Six-thousand students! Southwest Conference Football! *And the nearest known sin was right in town!*

The Baker-produced production was unlike any theatrical experience of my life. I had never seen anything like it. And, anything like it I have seen since was influenced strongly by Baker. I had a chance to visit with him briefly afterwards. I was convinced that he was one of the rarest souls in captivity. And I was right.

With Zula's help I was able to get Baker's promise of some scholarship help if I proved to be a good student and would work hard in the theater. I assured him I could do all of that plus working in a church part-time. He should have no fear. I would work harder than any student had ever worked. I would blaze new trails and chart new courses in the theater. Just how I would work all that into a career in the ministry I had not yet finalized . . .

So I arrived at Baylor. And I almost left at the end of my first week. There were more students in the lounge of my dorm than we had enrolled at Wayland! I had never seen that many people in one place in my life. I felt lost and estranged. I hitch-hiked home every weekend that first year, partly to carry on a thriving romance, partly to avoid the misery of the multitude.

Gradually, Baylor cracked my shell. I began to get into the swing of campus activites, to make solid and lifelong friends. I organized another quartet and performed regularly all over the territory.

Paul Baker and I did not get on well at all. I lasted in his courses for two semesters. I felt that he was the most conceited man I had ever known. It was years later in serious counseling and self-evaluation that I came to realize his great strengths and why I felt so antagonistic toward him. *Paul Baker was the first person who ever let me know that he could see right through me.* He would not let me be anything less than my absolute best. When I tried to bluff him, he'd nail me. I was used to being applauded, not criticized. I have had many regrets in my life. Chief among them is that I did not see clearly what Paul Baker was up to, how he could have helped me. I could not affirm that for ten more years.

Baylor did allow me to meet and work with many other special "shaping" folks. Martha "Barkie" Barkema took me into the Baylor Bards and Rhapsody in White, a coed touring choir. We had more fun than any other group on the campus, I feel certain. She gave me free voice lessons, got me some presidential scholarship money, helped me get a part in the campus opera one year and, in general, let me help her run things. One year I got to be the tour manager. I loved working with her.

Once, I gave her heart failure in the middle of a concert! We were singing in Livingston, Texas, as a preparatory road trip, a "singing shake-down cruise." I had a solo part in an anthem we had been singing for two or three years. It was a quiet phrase with the choir humming a steady chord behind it. The choir would go *hmmmm*. Then, I'd sing: "And the glory of the Lord is risen upon thee . . ."

We came to that part that night and Barkie gave the *hmmm* sign and the choir *hmmmmmed*. She looked to her right on the back row to her faithful soloist for the standard good job he faithfully and regularly performed. I opened my mouth and sang forth! What I heard myself sing I had *never heard*! I don't know where it came from! It came out: "And the ransomed of the Lord shall see and believe it . . ."

The choir nearly bit their *hmmmmm* off trying not to laugh! Barkie snapped a look at me that would have killed the only palm at the oasis! I shrugged my eyebrows and grinned bleakly. I was not responsible! I had never heard it myself! Don't look at me!

Then she got tickled. It took her four or five seconds to compose herself and the choir. Then she moved on into the remainder of the anthem. I was relieved. But every few bars she'd look up at me with a twinkle in her eye that said: "You crazy character!"

Baylor was the scene of a monumental religious awakening in the spring of 1946. In that event a nightly revival meeting was held, camp-meeting style, under a large tent on the intramural football field—right in the center of the campus. There was preaching and personal testifying and sharing of religious experiences. Many of the campus leaders were touched during these meetings. One was Charles Wellborn, a debater and scholar of the first magnitude. He made a startling public decision that week to become a Christian, which sent a shock wave through the campus. On the heels of Wellborn's new-found faith in God, there came a tidal wave of athletes, beauty queens, accountants, teachers, and fraternity/sorority types.

These young people began sharing this experience all over Texas and surrounding states. Several of the young men, Wellborn included, committed their lives to the ministry and began preaching immediately. Baptists ordain anyone willing! They were preaching in the largest churches in the state; they were holding Billy Graham-style crusades in stadiums and coliseums. This was three years before Billy Graham erupted in the city of San Francisco in his first nationally publicized revival meeting.

It was referred to as the Youth Revival Movement in Texas. The response was awesome. Young people preaching to young people, singing to young people, talking and counseling with young people. And young people responding in staggering numbers with amazing results. Baylor was the hub of the movement, but there were similar experiences breaking out on other campuses all over the state.

I was part of the third college generation after the

great Youth Revival Movement. I had been strongly influenced by this movement—Hoyt Mulkey had come to Jacksonville as part of such a revival. Since he had done this, I wanted to do this, also. I began to work with the teams of young people going to various churches, largely using music and entertainment at after-church social and fellowship gatherings. I played the ukulele so much that my right forefinger nearly calloused over! I sang the classic songs written for the movement: "Longing for Jesus"; "Turn Your Eyes Upon Jesus"; "It Took a Miracle." I was out on the weekends for three-day revivals during the school year. Occasionally, I'd spend a weekend with a church group on retreat— two or three days of concentrated time together at a campsite or conference center.

One summer I stayed on the road for twelve continuous weeks in revival after revival. I was in a number of states other than Texas. It was in such a revival in Memphis, Tennessee, that I met Eleanor Wilson. We met on Sunday morning. By Thursday night I was convinced that someday she'd be my wife. I was right!

She sang in the youth choir in her church—the Lamar Heights Baptist Church. I was supposed to be leading the music that morning, but I was sitting in the audience due to a typical "comedy-of-errors" in my life. I had shipped my clothes for the revival to Memphis in a footlocker. A good Baylor friend in the church was to have them pressed by the time I arrived on Saturday evening. I got there to discover that he'd forgotten the clothes. They were still at the cleaners . . .

So I borrowed one of his suits. I looked like the guy who starred in Andy Griffith's "What It Was Was Football!" He was six inches shorter than I. My arms were a broomhandle-length longer than his. I know folks thought that I had been baptized last Sunday—*in my suit*! So I sat out in the congregation trying to shrink by six inches.

Sitting there embarrassed to death, I spied Eleanor in the choir. I was done in from the start. What a beauty! I remembered a brief conversation with my inner self in which I declared: "If she were at Baylor, I'd date her or die trying!" After the service, she came straight toward me. I was palpitating. I had noticed her smiling at me throughout the service; it was too good to be true . . .

"I'm Eleanor Wilson," she introduced. "And I'm coming to Baylor this fall!" I was ready to die trying! Then, I thought I'd die *without* trying! She turned and introduced her steady boyfriend to me. He'd been sitting right in front of me during the entire service. Guess who she'd been smiling at? And guess who she hadn't?

But he didn't have a chance after she got to Baylor. It was easily the greatest year of my life to that point. I beamed every time I saw her. I couldn't see enough of her. It was a special time for two terribly naive people. We thought we were doing the best job possible in getting ready for marriage and family. We had a smooth relationship without conflict or dissension. It was later to become obvious to us that we had not learned to communicate our ideas and feelings about each other, about ourselves. We were eventually to know sheer pain of the first magnitude . . .

But, for now, we were having fun. She watched, cheering from the sidelines, as I rode the crest of campus activity. I was to become a yell leader for the athletic events, was already quite active in the campus religious life. My most consuming interest, however, turned out to be the quartet I helped to form—"The Troubadours."

We sang a broad variety of music. Between the four of us we played twenty-seven instruments! We parodied popular musicians of the day—Elvis Presley, Harry Belafonte, The Four Freshmen, The Ink Spots. Three or four nights each week we entertained for banquets and other functions all over Texas and Oklahoma. One week we made four trips—the shortest of which was *180 miles one way*! We'd get back to the campus about 2:30 or 3:00 in the morning, drag out for classes, leave after lunch, drive for half-a-forever, and repeat the process. I managed the schedule and expenses for the group. Each of the four of us paid for his school expenses by entertaining with this group.

Most of my later touch with spontaneous humor grew out of "fronting" for the quartet, being the person to announce and introduce all the numbers. We mixed a good deal of comedy into our performances and got good mileage out of our own goofs. Our rehearsal time was usually in the car on the way to an engagement. We frequently performed a new number that evening that we had just concocted in the car!

These years gave me a superb opportunity to know and hone my skills as entertainer/speaker/minister. I was before church groups, company functions, civic clubs, school assemblies, college audiences. I have always loved the challenge of speaking to a "duke's mixture" of audiences in a varied set of circumstances. Those years gave me a lifetime of experience.

In retrospect, I was seeing the shape of my future life and life's work "through a glass darkly." What was intended to be only a way to pay college expenses was proving to be the perfect training ground. If I had served an apprenticeship in night clubs or other such places, my humor would have been shaped differently. But my launching pad was ideal. I was in and out of churches and other Christian gatherings—all of it in character with my sense of purpose and "calling."

Never had the scripture made so much sense to me: "All things work together for good to those who love God" (Rom. 8:28, RSV). I did love God. And I loved Eleanor. And I loved entertaining and leading in church work.

Things were definitely working together for good . . .

FOLLOW THE LEADER, BUT WATCH YOUR STEP!

In one month, three major events occurred in my life: I graduated from college; I got married, and I took my first church staff job. I wasn't ready for any of the three!

Most of my college education was in developing social skills, not in intellectual pursuits. I attended classes I did not study for; I chose professors who were not the more difficult and demanding teachers; I took the maximum cuts allowed, did the minimum work required. I stayed on for one additional quarter just to get enough grade points to graduate with an even C average. I worked hard at not working hard!

One month after I got a Bachelor of Arts degree, I got a lovely wife, Eleanor. We were typical for our era, I think. We thought you found the right person, got a job, rented a house, and marriage would take care of itself. We managed to coast along in "honeymoon gear" for the next few years. We were later to learn that what we thought we were planting as flowers turned out to be weeds . . .

Perry, our first son, was born on our ten-month anniversary. Almost from the beginning, we were not just a *couple*—we were either pregnant or a family. It is a tough assignment to be asked to pass "family" before you've had the introductory course of "couple."

My first job was as youth minister of the First Baptist Church in Waco, Texas, just up the street from Baylor University about six blocks. Many of my classmates at Baylor were members of this fine church during their college years. I had the somewhat awkward task of trying to lead my peers. I now know that I was better at attracting a crowd than I was at doing something constructive with them after they were assembled. For the time being, however, it was college-life extended, excitement around every corner.

One of my areas of expertise was in reaching out to the teenagers of the church. We had a tendency as a church to be awed by six hundred college members who filled a large segment of our space and took up a large chunk of our time and energy— while we virtually ignored the high school and junior high school young people. They had to live off the leftovers of our time and resources. I depended rather heavily on my college council (a group of college students who planned most of the activities with the college membership) to direct us in our ministry to the campus. I spent most of my time with the teenagers.

That was obviously more comfortable for me. They were younger by several years. They were more easily led by a person my age than were my college friends. I could rally them at the drop of a hat for a swim party, for a backyard social, for a fellowship time after church, for a retreat or camp, for a fun time.

As youth minister, I had the responsibility for

helping to select the teachers and leaders for our educational ministry in the teenage and college levels of the church. I was woefully unprepared to lead adults. I could not rally laymen who worked at full-time jobs in the community to be as enthusiastic about my great leadership as I could the impressionable juniors in high school! I was not *then* and am not *now* a well-organized human being. I was asking people to invest their lives and their energies in the ministry of our church to do things I was not thinking *through* or even sometimes thinking *about*! There were no picket-parades outside my office, but from the vantage point of more training and more maturity, I have come to see that the church was performing one of its greatest acts of charity in not sending me away to sing to cows on the prairie somewhere!

I've read that last paragraph several times and choose not to reword it. It is probably too harsh in some areas and may not be honest enough in some others. The main point is that I did accomplish some good with the youth of the church, but I was not a quality leader. What began to soak in on me was that I was experiencing mass frustration in quiet solitude. I assumed it was because a "prophet is without honor in his own country," so I began to feel that I could be a better prophet in another country. I got a chance to move to another church in a similar position and took it. I left Waco after twenty months that had been enjoyable, had been enlightening, had convinced me that I could *really* make it in another setting.

I became youth minister at the Gaston Avenue Baptist Church in Dallas, Texas.

I doubt that there have been many churches in the history of organizing for youth ministry that could

match the leadership manpower and commitment of
this fine church. I was to work with the adult
leadership in coordinating our ministry to about two
hundred teenagers and some college-age youth. We
had a good budget to work with; we had a staff of
folks who buried their lives in teaching and working
with the youth. A few of these people had been
working in Sunday School and other organizations of
the church for twenty and thirty years. I had
overwhelming resources with which to work.

And I was overwhelmed.

Again, I spent most of my time with the young
people and tried to gain their allegiance and
followship. I remember very well one night having
one of the group call my house about 6:00 to see if
there were something we might do together that
night. We talked for a few minutes; he thought the
Schwettmans might let us use their backyard for a
volley ball game and general "be together time." I
had him check it out, promised to get soft drinks
iced down, and set the time for 7:30. The word got
around like fire in a haybarn. I arrived at 7:15 to
unload the half-ton of Dr. Peppers. At 7:30 *eighty*
high-schoolers piled into the Schwettmans' backyard!

Frankly, what happened with me during those
months in Dallas was almost predictable. I simply
became the oldest adolescent in the gang. I did not
seem to fit in unusually well in my own high school
years. I could not go to dances or movies or
swimming parties. I did not date or feel like part of
the "movers and doers." At Gaston Avenue Baptist
Church I worked so hard at becoming one of the
teenagers *that I became one of the teenagers.*

Adult leaders were rightfully (and sometimes
frightfully) concerned that I was not giving
concentrated leadership to the adults who had

invested their lives in working with young people in the church. I seemed to feel that as long as there were teachers for Sunday School and leaders for the other organized activities of the church, I was then free to spend all my time with the youth themselves. We did have a large attendance; we did have busyness and activity; we did have growth of numbers of young people. What we did not have was directed growth in spiritual maturity and a sense of real mission about our work.

Our second son, Toby, was born in the beginning of our second year in Dallas. The family was growing; the demands were increasing for my participation in child-rearing and managing the household. I suffered from three basic shortcomings at that time that were to bring me painfully face to face with myself before too long . . .

First, I assumed the attitude that women were to raise the children and look after the house; men were to earn the income, and provide for the basic economic necessities, repair the plumbing, and decide which car to buy. I just left Eleanor with the task of *upbringing* what we had *forthbrought!* It was also easy for me to fall into this category because I really did not think I had it in me to be a decent father and husband. Even *now* that is hard to admit about myself *then* . . .

Second, I was not competently trained to deal with the combination of demands made on me professionally. In essence, a bicycle mechanic was being called upon to launch a rocket. I saw a chance in two large church positions to jump over seminary training right into "the big time." I could not deal with the family counseling responsibilities, with the adult leadership tasks, with the theological questions being raised by bright and inquisitive young people. I merely quoted by rote, like gospel songs learned while standing at the end of an upright piano, simple solutions and pat answers that I had heard throughout my life. I did not know how to respond from experiential faith, from personal commitment.

Third, I allowed myself to substitute a busy schedule for hard work. I found excuses to sit at my desk in the evenings, to have serious conferences with young people after supper, to have something going on constantly which substituted for an organized approach to my work and for meaningful time with my family.

When you are running from your role as father and husband, you run from your wife and children. When you run from your responsibilities and work, you run from the people who could help you the most. When you run from the truth about yourself as an incompetent professional, you run in a never-ending maze of busyness and activity.

I had to face all that. And I had to face myself and some painful and shameful truths. It was a sifting and pruning time for me. I was in serious trouble on several fronts.

Then, I met Harles Cone, the seminary student. I had already known Harles Cone, the high school classmate, back in Jacksonville, Texas. He was one year behind me in school and a delight to know. He was out of college and now a student at Southwestern Baptist Theological Seminary in Fort Worth, Texas. He was one of a team of four college and seminary students leading our church in a summer youth revival in July of 1960.

One afternoon he and I were across the hall from my office in the fluorescent-lit church library. He exclaimed: "Oh, you have *Barclay!*" "Who?" I asked. "Barclay!" he repeated.

And we, indeed, did. William Barclay was a
Scottish scholar of the New Testament, specifically of
its Greek backgrounds. He had written a series of
commentaries on the New Testament in very
readable, layman's language. Harles proceeded to
tell me all the benefits he had gained from the study
of this great and good man's great and good work. I
was fascinated.

That night, I took home a copy of Barclay's
commentary on the Gospel of John, Volume 1. In
reading just the introduction to the volume, I heard
bells ring, saw lights flash, and vibrated inside like
Isaiah in the temple in the throes of a major vision!
Quite frankly, it was the first time in my life I felt that
someone knew anything about the Bible that I might
not already know! The possibility of studying that sort
of stuff further whetted my appetite. It was painfully
obvious that only seminary work would satisfy the
hunger.

Put my self-discovery together with my Barclay-
discovery, and you have all the ingredients of a
major decision. Add a liberal portion of confrontation
from superiors and church leaders trying to tell me I
was on the verge of vocational bankruptcy, and you
have the element of *timing*. Understand how I
dreaded failure and how I wanted to prove my ability
and live out my sense of calling—sins, goofs,
inadequacies and all—and you have what the
prophets of the Old Testament called "the voice of
God."

This time I needed to resign and get on to a new
place—not so I could hide but so I could *seek*. In
that spirit and with that certain knowledge, I did not
go to seminary to learn the outline of Nahum or the
four points of Paul's theology of Gentile evangelism.
I would learn those, and I did. I did not go for any

other reason than to learn about myself—as person, as minister, as husband, as father, as an adult responsible-for-my-gifts. I would later sit in class like a beggar with an alms cup, like a blind man feeling his way down a dirt path with a piece of tree limb. I would absorb and digest and gourge and question and debate and challenge and hurt and bleed internally and grow.

And find myself.

That is what lay ahead of me at Southern Seminary. Because that is what lay within me!

THE UNMASKING MARVEL

No life is without its pain and hurt. I've had my share. In fact, I've had enough to spread around!

My greatest pain came from hurting the person who brought me the greatest joy—my wife Eleanor. After four years of marriage and two remarkable sons, we came as close to losing a marriage as you can come. Rhea Gray was rain on my desert!

A sketchy outline of the rise and fall of your typically male-dominated marriage, if you please . . .

Eleanor and I met in college. We had two years of courting, dating, courting, engagement, courting, waiting, courting, courting, courting. Through it all, no arguments, no fusses, no slammed-down phones. More than harmony—*unison!* In Eleanor's words: "We *both* loved Grady!" True.

Her background was from a family of tranquillity. I came right from the family war zone! I was always in conflict with my parents; she was rarely out of sync with her folks. Her basic view of marriage was essentially: "If you love each other, you don't fight!" So she always agreed with me.

I loved being not only king of the mountain but

87

also the sovereign of our universe. I was not a benevolent dictator. I intimidated; I belittled; I erased the blackboard of her personality with a wet rag! I then wrote what I pleased . . .

Without knowing it, I had taken advantage of her will to please me. I grew to dislike her for letting me get away with it.

We were living in Seminary Village at Southern Baptist Theological Seminary in Louisville— Apartment S-9. For your typical lousy marriage, this was a choice location! Paint was peeling; steam radiator pipes played the Doxology; through the walls you could hear your neighbors chew oatmeal! It was our second year, our fourteenth month, in S-9 and in bad trouble . . .

For some time we had been cordial but not close; we had mumbled "I love you," but it had not crackled with vitality in ages. One night we got honest. Maybe a better way to put it would be that we started verbalizing our pain without yelling or trying to bruise. I said that I didn't see any hope for us, that I couldn't go on like this. She sat looking at me like a flood victim . . .

Then I mentioned the word *divorce*. Suddenly, her eyes lit up like a dalmatian hearing the fire alarm! Everything about her said, "Bottom of the ninth, two men on, two out . . ." Driven by fear and determination, she catapulted from the house the next morning to the office of Rhea Gray.

I need to tell you a bit about Rhea. He was a graduate student at our seminary, working toward a doctorate in Psychology of Religion, more recently referred to as Pastoral Care. He was working his way through school as Baptist campus minister at the University of Louisville and as director of a marriage and family counseling center in New Albany,

Indiana—right across the Ohio River from Louisville. We knew him socially and casually.

At this time in our lives, neither Eleanor nor I had ever known even one person who had "gone for counseling." I had then and have since then heard the whole field of psychology and psychiatry held up to ridicule by ministers and other church folks.

Rhea received Eleanor with compassion, with understanding, and with Christian love. He told her many good things about herself and about the potential for our marriage. The only snag in the deal was that he encouraged her to tell me that she had seen him for help.

Divorce might have easier.

Eleanor took one whole week to work up the courage to tell me that she had seen Rhea. Her timing was terrible! We were driving down a Louisville street on our way home from church one Sunday night. I made a comment that I wished we could go back to the happy days of college dating and start over again. That was the moment she chose to tell me in one cascading blurt that she had "beentoseeRheaGrayforcounselingandhesayshecan helpus!" I, stunned, said, "WHAT!"

She, nervously, repeated more understandably, "I've been to see Rhea Gray for counseling and he says he can help us!" Last paragraph, I mentioned *timing.* Being interpreted: I was driving a normal-roof Volkswagen; suddenly, it had a sunroof! Swerving and yelling, I blew my cool! That's what I mean by poor timing . . .

We arrived at S-9. She took one child; I took the other. With diaper bags, Bible, books, purse, and other family-at-church paraphernalia, we made our way tensely up the walk under trees doing their best to screen our conflict from the neighbors. I put my half of the dependents in his bed, put down a diaper bag, picked up a sackful of garbage, and left. Later, Eleanor said she thought that was symbolic.

I went out to the apartment dumpster and threw in the bag of garbage. I weighed for a moment the possibility of getting in with it. For the next two or three hours, I wandered around the Village, punting stumps. It was out in the open now. Someone knew I had a problem. What was more nearly the truth, I had really come to see for myself that I had a problem.

Trashless and crushed, I opened the door of S-9 to see Eleanor sitting terrified on the sofa. I burst into tears and told her she had done the very best thing for us, for me. I took her in my arms and cried as hard as I had at age eleven when my mother overheard me cussing with my next-door neighbor out in our garage one afternoon. A while later, I looked up Rhea's number and called him. It was almost midnight.

He agreed to see me the next morning at his home. At 9:30 Eleanor and I walked into his home and sat down at his kitchen table. Grace and redemption sat across the sugar bowl and jelly dish from me in the form of Rhea Gray.

For the next two months I saw Rhea every week, as did Eleanor. He never told me what they talked about; he never told her what *we* talked about. The beautiful thing that began to happen was that we started talking *with* each other—*really* talking with each other. Out of it all, each of us learned a life-changing lesson . . .

Eleanor learned that when we met she had been a person with a personality, with abilities, and with every reason to celebrate her own gifts and resources. For me, she had given up her own wishes just to please me, to make *us* happy. The sad fact was that the more she ceased to be herself, the less I liked/loved her. She began getting in touch with her own strengths and gifts. She has grown as much, if not more, than any person I have known in the past twenty years. I have come to love and appreciate her so much more as an independent soul with a mind of her own, with interests of her own, even with friends of her own. She is at the opposite end of the spectrum from the "submissive wife." And I love it!

The biggest breakthrough about myself also came through Rhea Gray. I told him the darkest secrets of my life. I shared things with him I had never told anyone. I confessed sins and *sin.* I admitted insecurities down behind this great extroverted front of mine. He heard it all, carefully guided me into conversations about deeper aspects of it all. Then came the golden moment . . .

He told me that he saw me as a person who had spent most of my life wearing a mask so people wouldn't see what I'm really like. In the process of hiding behind my mask, he saw that a real person had grown up behind that mask! He said, "When you get acquainted with the person you *really* are, you're going to love him!" For the very first time in my life, I was able to begin to believe that I really had some strengths, some abilities, some worth. I didn't have to earn it. I didn't have to prove it. I *did* have to accept it! Only then could I begin to share it . . .

. . . and, it has been the unfolding story of my continuing struggle to be the person God created me to be.

I did not turn the emotional corner of my life in two months of marital counseling. Rhea was superb in what he was called on to do; he could most surely have helped me much further if we had taken the time. However, it was a healthy thing that I had some space for a season, some time to absorb what Eleanor and I were busy learning about our life together. My big struggle with my personal turmoil was to come later.

I need to tell you one thing more about my relationship to Rhea . . .

In 1968 he called me from Chicago. By that time, he was president/director of a charitable foundation. His call was to pursue the possibility of my coming on the staff as his associate. I decided with Eleanor that it was just not really the place for me. I declined the invitation with enormous regret. I would have loved working up close with Rhea.

I tell you that to bring the story of his belief in me full circle. The incredible gift he gave me was to know my life so well, know my secrets and my inadequacies, and still offer me a post on his staff. Rhea gave me many gifts in our relationship. The greatest was a feeling that there was something within this Nutt worth unshelling and sharing . . .

AFFIRMED: A FOUNDATION

Napoleon met his Waterloo; I met Samuel Southard!

His nickname is *Sim*. When I met him, he was teaching Psychology of Religion at my seminary. He had a reputation for being caustic, confrontal, cut-to-the-core, hard to fool. When you work as hard at being lovable as I had always worked, you steadfastly avoid the Sim Southards of life! I got him with both barrels!

Each student in the basic divinity course was required to have a course in Psychology of Religion. In it, we dealt with the many counseling and pastoral tasks of the minister. We were brought to a solid awareness of our role in caring for persons during the great crises of life—death, conflict, illness, etc. Classes were held on only four days each week—Tuesday through Friday. On Fridays we had small groups of eight, with each group meeting with a certified pastoral counselor. My group was led by Southard himself . . .

The first time our Friday group met, we were asked individually to share some of our own hopes and desires in gaining insight from such a group. Most of us had never had a similar experience. Our comments around the circle were largely generalities. I had already figured Southard for a no-nonsense type; so, I laid out some specifics in pretty candid language.

I wanted to gain from the group some insights into why I felt as insecure as I did; why I had trouble speaking my honest opinions about situations, and why I wanted to get in touch with my real self. I remember one specific statement, "I want to know what really makes me tick!"

The next Tuesday Southard came down the hall between classes and spotted me reading the bulletin board. He walked over to me and said, "Have you had your flu shot yet?"

"No," I replied.

"Come on. We're going to get your flu shot . . ."

With that, he started walking across the campus toward the infirmary. I didn't want the shot. I certainly didn't want the flu! But his whole attitude said that he was interested in "what made me tick," not just my relation to the flu bug! I followed at his typical break-neck walking pace. Most of the good times we had talking, we had walking . . .

From the administration building bulletin board to the library building is about two hundred normal steps; we made it in about forty-seven. In those forty-seven huffing-puffing steps, Southard had pried the lid off my life. Another hundred steps or so, and we had reached the infirmary and at least two or three of my gravest fears. Shots accomplished, we resumed the walk and talk. By the time we had reached the bulletin board again, he said: "Would you like to talk about this further?"

I was a powder key waiting for the plunger to

ignite me. As earnestly as I have ever said anything in my life, I replied, "Yes."

We agreed on the next morning at 10:00, his office. I regarded it with bittersweet anticipation—I needed help. I was well aware that with Southard I couldn't play games.

If there be, in fact, *pivotal characters*, then it follows that there are also *pivotal moments*! *Example*: When you finally figure out how to find a square root! In Sim Southard's office on a Wednesday morning at 10:00, my pivotal character brought me to a pivotal moment . . .

I entered the office with my heart in my throat. I knew he could hear it. My palms were soggy. I was as flat as starched ironing. He greeted me warmly, sensitively. He had me take a seat.

He took a seat beside me, facing in the same direction, looking out the same window. In retrospect, that was a marvelous touch. It kept eye contact at a minimum, allowed me to feel and deal with delicate information and feelings without being stared at. He didn't have to prod much to get my avalanche rolling down the mountainside . . .

For the next forty minutes I dumped; I bled; I cried; I ached out loud! I left no conscious stone unturned, no shortcoming unconfessed, no fear unadmitted, no anguish unshared. I was, in fact, screaming quietly . . .

He allowed me to compose myself for a few moments. Our appointed time was drawing to a close. Then he asked an interesting question: "Grady, have you ever cried like this about yourself before?"

"No," I said.

"Have you talked about this with anyone before?"

"Not even with Eleanor," I replied.

"I don't see how you have held it all in *this long*! I don't see how you have kept your senses about you!"

When he made that statement, his voice seemed to break ever so slightly. Since we had both been facing in the same direction for the past forty minutes, I had not looked directly at him even once. I glanced over my left shoulder at Sim Southard, the "hard rock" of the psychology faculty, the flintheart of flinthearts. There he sat in his light tan suit, hearing my pain. What created my pivotal moment was this: *Sim Southard's suit front was soaked with tears!*

Compassion was wearing a soggy suit that day. It was a pivotal moment I have never lost, one I remember as though it were yesterday.

I am sure I must have seemed like a trailer on Southard's hitch for the next six months. I saw him regularly on a weekly basis for about the next three months. I signed up for an advanced course with him the next semester. He never let our closeness prevent him from being every bit the teacher. I recall one very explosive visit I had in his office . . .

We took a major test soon after I got into the counseling sessions with him. I made a grand score of 26 out of a possible 100! It was an essay test, involving a bit of judgment-call on the part of the grader. I felt that I had been wronged and that the score should have been higher. I almost tore the door off its hinges as I burst in on Sim. I was getting in touch with my hostile feelings, my deep anger in life. Without knowing it at the time, I think what I was doing on this visit was venting some feelings where I knew I'd be safe. After all, if *he* had cried when *I* cried, surely he could respond honestly to my other emotions as well. I gave him a chance with anger . . .

"I can't believe you'd have a dim-wit grading for you! I turn in a paper I worked hard on, studied hard for, used big words in, and you give me a *26*! A lousy *26*!"

Captain Cool aimed his artillery calmly. He glanced over the paper quietly while I boiled. I was feeling very much the he-man dealing up-front with my shattered ego; no more Mr. Nice Guy for me! Finally he looked up . . .

"You got a better grade than you deserve. This is a lousy paper. You totally overlooked . . ." On and on and on went the blistering indictment. I had no hole to crawl in, no feathers left to help me fly. I collapsed in a chair. I stared at him in hurt and disbelief.

"And you can't make the grade with me," he went on, "by buying me lunch and buttering me up with friendship. You're a far better student than this paper indicates, and I will give you only what you earn in this class. I won't tolerate second-rate stuff out of you. Give me a decent paper—you'll get a decent grade! Understand?"

I went down the hall like a balloon released after blow-up, directionless and numb. The wind had been knocked out of me.

So I buckled down to the task of working at my grades. In that course I pulled out a C +, no minor miracle considering the poor start I had made. In his advanced elective I made an A, one of the highest grades in a class of fifty-six students. My entire academic pilgrimage took a major about-face, thanks to Southard, and my average came up almost an entire letter grade in the last two years of a four-year program.

It was in one of the Friday small-group times that I had another of those incredible breakthrough moments. We finished the class time in good spirits and headed for our corner of the cafeteria to have our regularly scheduled "brown-bag" lunch. A most interesting thing was happening to our group—we'd get together in the lunchroom and rehash the supervised class sessions.

It was in one of those sessions one day that I was confronted over several brown bags with the fact that my humor was so hostile. I tried to laugh it off, but they were serious. They admitted to being bruised, to being threatened, to being angry frequently with the way I put people down and "jokingly" ran over their feelings. I was totally unaware of this! I honestly did not know I had a hostile bone in my body! I just made fun, had crazy comebacks for folks, teased them, and in general, felt "happy go lucky." The group put my humor under the microscope and did a real dissecting job on it . . .

. . . and I ricocheted off that session into Southard's office . . .

He helped me see that my humor was a marvelous defense for me. I could tell people unpleasant things and express my true feelings, but disguise them in such a way that I didn't have to risk being rejected by my target. *Example*: I might see you in a plaid coat. You'd ask me what I thought of your coat. I'd say, "Lie down and I'll play you a game of checkers!" You'd say, "You don't like my coat?" I'd respond, "You can't take a joke!" I'd laugh at you, walk away, and leave you in a heap. I would have told you what I thought of your outlandish jacket. I would have avoided being put in an unpleasant relationship with you. I had not risked being rejected by you.

This is the way I had spent my life. I was small, rather frail, and unathletic. I loved music and art and reading and other safe things in the non-contact areas. I learned how to defend myself around the stronger and more physical types by being quick with a quip. You might be able to out-wrestle me, but you'd have a hard time out-talking me!

It was Sim Southard who helped me get the hostility out of my humor. I do not claim to be totally healed, but I am vastly improved. I still do not like to confront anyone with unpleasant opinions or feelings, but I can do that better than before Southard! And my fun has been free to become real fun, my humor to be free of anger and ridicule. Much of what we laugh at is at another person's expense. That has come to pain me greatly when I see it happen.

Therefore, I come to my place in life, my calling in life, using humor as a valuable tool of communication. I find myself more nearly able to *share* something rather than having to *prove* something. My clay was never in better hands than those of my great molder, Sim Southard.

Interesting sequel . . .

. . . in the spring of my senior year in seminary, I was planning to graduate, remain as pastor of the church I served during my last two years in school, and take one or two additional courses in counseling and pastoral ministries as a "special student." These courses would be for non-credit, taken on a post-graduate basis. Sim took me to lunch one day . . .

"What are your plans after graduation?

"I plan to stay at Graefenburg, enjoy some time out of the academic rat race, and probably take a couple of courses as a special student."

"Why as a *special student*?" he inquired.

"Well, I think my grades are probably borderline enough that I'd have a tough time getting into graduate school."

"I've been checking your grades already," he said.
"You have the qualifications if you can pass the
entrance exams into the program. I'd like for you to
consider doing a graduate degree with me . . ."

"With *you*?" I almost yelled it!

"With me," he smiled/said.

Now, you cannot imagine how far that moves
from the day we almost came to blows after I made
a 26 on one of his tests! I had been asked to step
from the also-rans to the front of the class! I just had
to sit there and stare at my barbecue sandwich . . .

My mentor, my encourager, my teacher, my
friend, my supporter, my affirmer. Sim Southard.

In more ways than you can possibly know, I owe
him my very life . . .

HUGS LIFTED ME

Each member of my family—Eleanor, Perry , and Toby—will probably agree that two of the best years of our lives were spent at Graefenburg, Kentucky. I was pastor of the Graefenburg Baptist Church, Route 2, Waddy, Kentucky, for two years—my last two years in seminary.

And you pronounce it: GRAFF-in-burg . . .

The community is situated almost geographically at the center of a line between Louisville and Lexington; it is on the very edge of the famous bluegrass region of Kentucky. The local economy is based on tobacco farming. The folks are mostly farm folks. Some work in Frankfort, the state capitol, either in private business or for the state government.

I went there as pastor with limited pastoral-type experience. I had been on three different church staffs up to that point, but I had not had the kind of pastoral experience this church would both demand from me and teach me!

It started off like it was going to continue—casual and comfortable. The men of the church came to S-9, Seminary Village, in a cattle truck to move the new preacher into the parsonage. The truck was full to overflowing with the accumulated possessions of a young seminarian and his family. Clark Dawson, one of the senior deacons of the church, stood in the yard of the parsonage observing the unloading, propped on his walking cane. He remarked in his typical droll fashion: "Next time we get a preacher, we better get one that's poor! These rich ones have too much stuff to lug around!" The luggers laughed with Clark and the new, "rich" preacher. Little did I know at the time how rich I was going to feel as pastor of this church!

Few things give a country church pleasure to equal that of "breaking in" a city-type preacher. They absolutely loved watching me try to learn about heifers, milking machines, "toppin' tobacco," plant beds, squirrel and groundhog hunting, and all the rest. I marveled at the way they could give directions: "Just go over to the big hill past Odell and turn back away from Evergreen. Poole's place is just before the Interstate on your right." Once you found Odell's place and knew where Evergreen was, you were alright. It wasn't long before I could give out country-style directions, too.

My sons loved the country. We raised our own little beagle pup and had one of the fine rabbit hunters in the territory. We even got to run him with Rondal Dawson's trial dog occasionally.

The boys watched the farmers plow, milk, harvest tobacco, and shoot basketball at the goal on the side of the barn. They wore little hightop farm shoes, never thought of putting on anything but jeans (even for Sunday services!), and could tell a bull from a cow across the pasture!

We moved into the parsonage in June of 1962. The parsonage had been built in the Depression with scrap lumber for about $500, as I recall. Odell Smith said you could "throw a cat through the cracks" before they fixed it up. I'm glad they fixed it up!

Boots Smith called to tell me that I could have fresh vegetables if I could get there to pick them. Odell Smith raised the best corn in the area, and we got all we could eat. Earl Bailey gave me part of his first green bean pickings.

I hunted rabbits and squirrels with Rondal Dawson; I hunted groundhogs with Bill Wingate. I roamed freely over the church field with a feeling of belonging like I have rarely experienced in my life.

Etha Dawson could cook biscuits like no one I've ever known. I used to go by on Monday mornings after my Frankfort bank-deposit run and have cold biscuits with Etha. She knew I'd be coming on Mondays and probably fixed a few extras . . .

I visited in hospitals. I called on folks in the field and at the house. I tended to a variety of problems here and there. I probably learned as much at Graefenburg as I did at Southern Seminary in those two years.

Preaching was special for me. I loved to get at the business of preparing sermons and leading in worship. I was not one of the greatest preachers in the world, but I loved it as much as the great ones. I especially loved the response of the congregation. I tried especially hard to preach to children, youth, *and* adults.

I conducted my first funeral on Tuesday after I arrived on Saturday. I saw marital calamity first-hand. I saw businessmen and farmers struggle with finances and with each other. I was at peace like I had never been at peace . . .

In the midst of my work at Graefenburg, I was undergoing many changes due to my counseling and group sharing at the seminary. I drove forty-two miles each way four days each week to attend classes. My work was about eighty-four hours long, counting homework . . .

My first year as pastor ended at the end of my first year with Sim Southard, my third seminary year. Mixed with my joy as a pastor was the pain of self-discovery. I had to deal almost daily with the paradox of turmoil and pain at school, joy and growing fulfillment at Graefenburg. It was a heavy load to "tote," but I shouldered it and pressed on.

I finished my third year in seminary. I finished my first year as pastor. That summer nearly finished me . . .

A very personal matter almost drove me into Great Depression II. I got to the point by July 1 that I could not get any drive going, could not tend to folks, could not bear any more of anyone's concern and care, could hardly get my chin off my chest. I saw the church's vitality gradually wane as my leadership involvement trickled down to a drip. By October of my senior year in seminary, I had reached the dregs in my bucket!

On a Saturday night, Eleanor and I drove into Louisville with Babe and Edith Rogers for a good steak dinner at one of the nicer restaurants downtown. I don't know how we got into it, but during the meal I began to share some of my experiences of the past several months—the heaviness and the misery of my personal life. Babe, one of my deacons and church kingpins, could hardly believe what I was telling him. He said: "I never dreamed that you were going through anything like that!" I nestled in the comforting warmth of those good friends like I had once snuggled into Grandma's feather bed.

The trip back to Graefenburg was a breath of fresh air for me, for Eleanor; I'm sure it was special for Babe and Edith. We talked deeply and honestly. They really got under my load with me and gave me some relief.

Later that night, I found myself tossing and turning in the bed. I glanced at the luminous clockface and saw it was 3:00 a.m. I got up and rinsed my face in the bathroom, stretched and twisted my body a bit to get the circulation going, drank a glass of milk, and then sat down in the nightlight-lit living room to ponder, to pray.

And then it came to me. I knew what must be done.

The next morning I asked the choir not to "robe up." I asked them just to have a seat in the congregation. After a hymn and the offertory, I stood for about forty-five minutes to share the turmoil of the past several months of my life. I shared everything that I felt I could share with them, confessing at the conclusion my inadequacies as their pastor. I felt that they had been shortchanged in terms of my time to look after them and the general routines of running the church effectively and with consistency.

Baptist and evangelical churches in general have a tradition that is very special to them. Throughout the revival movement and subsequent emphases in worship on repentance and public confession of sin, there has been an opportunity at the conclusion of worship for an altar call, frequently referred to as an "invitation" or "decision service." I felt impressed to use this form familiar to me and my church to say symbolically what I had been verbalizing to the congregation.

I told them that I was going to step down from the

pulpit to the altar of the church. As I did so, I was simultaneously going to do two things. First, I was going to recommit my life to God, to be more open to His strength and direction, to be the person He was leading me to be. Second, I was going to recommit my life to the church, to be the kind of pastor I knew I could be, the kind of pastor they needed and deserved. I asked for their prayers and understanding; I asked for their forgiveness. I was crying profusely.

I walked down the steps to my right, then walked back across to the center of the altar area and turned to face the congregation. I planned to stand there quietly for a few moments and then pronounce the benediction and leave. It was then that I was grabbed by Kyle Milton . . .

I need to stop here and tell you about Kyle Milton. He was a deacon and a farmer. And, I think, in that order. He was about five feet, eight inches tall, stocky, stout, always pleasant and jovial. He was married to the unchallenged best cook in several counties, Erma. If *Life Magazine* ever publishes a special issue on "American Grandparents," Kyle and Erma should be the couple on the cover. Without a pitchfork!

Kyle taught me to chew tobacco. He grew, twisted, cut, and cured his own. We'd sit on his porch and swing and chew. It was the easiest habit I ever gave up! But Kyle loved the stuff; you hardly ever saw him without a plug in his jaw.

Kyle could do most anything around the farm. He could even weld. One of my memories of him was on a Sunday morning when he came by after the services to tell me he'd enjoyed the sermon. I noticed spots all over his glasses. The spots were not light-colored, like raindrops or splattered milk. The spots were dark gray, more like the color of ash. I asked him about the spots. He blushed; Erma chuckled and gave him an affectionate jab with her elbow. He confessed to having tried to do a quick welding job on a piece of machinery the day before but didn't want to go to the trouble of rounding up his welding goggles. So, he lit the torch and started his repair job, sparks flying. Some of them, molten steel, hit the glasses and pitted the surface. Kyle wore them for several months just like that until he finally got a new pair.

This Sunday morning Kyle couldn't have seen well out of *un*pitted glasses. He was weeping as openly as I.

I was facing the congregation. Kyle caught me from the left side. His left arm went across my chest, his right arm across my shoulder blades. His head was buried on my left shoulder. His hands were clasped on my other one. He held me in front of the whole church and just sobbed.

Almost before you could have caught your breath, the entire church was at the altar with me, all in tears, all reaching to try to get just one hand on me somewhere. Most of them managed.

For about ten or fifteen minutes we just stood there in a clump. Sniffs, nose-blows, open tears, arms around each other, handholding, peopleholding . . .

Then I started—feebly—to sing the Doxology. "Praise God from Whom all blessings flow . . ."

Some moments you never forget. Some moments you easily rekindle. Some moments make you what you are "foreverafter." This was one of those incredible moments . . .

Today, many years later, I still live forty-two miles from my other home, Graefenburg. I still go back to visit, to keep touch with the folks. I have been back to speak several times, to participate in a funeral or two. I drive by frequently on I-64 and can see the steeple of the church and the community nestled in the crook of Goose Creek, snuggled up to the rolling hills of near-bluegrass country. I can still mist up as I recall what a difference it made one Sunday for a young pastor to be hugged by that church . . .

   . . . all at once!

UNTIL YOU'VE SAID YES,
YOU HAVEN'T SAID NO

Bill Lancaster is most surely the reason I am doing what I am doing today. I don't blame him; I thank him!

I graduated from seminary in June of 1964. I received my divinity degree on Friday; I received the key to my office at the seminary on Monday at 8:00 a.m. I was now the Director of Alumni Affairs and Assistant to the President of The Southern Baptist Theological Seminary, Louisville, Kentucky. My calling card was nine inches long . . .

I was responsible for two major areas of work in the administrative structure of the seminary. First, I was to direct all our efforts in student recruitment— visiting with and otherwise encouraging college students who were considering our seminary as the place for their theological education. I normally traveled from eight to ten days per month visiting college campuses all over the nation. It was delightful!

Second, I was responsible for the alumni functions of the seminary—reunion meetings, alumni fund-raising, placement services for graduating students as well as graduates. I tended to these chores mostly at my desk in Louisville.

I knew almost within a year that I was not really institutional material. I think my superiors knew it in about two months! A mark of true Christian character on the part of the president of the seminary is that he did not call me in and ship me out!

I am not only disorganized—I am also scatterbrained! I do not get Project A finished before I start on Project B. I don't even keep to a budget at home, much less at the office. I thought long-range planning was when you planned what you were going to do after lunch! I am sure I drove the folks above me berserk!

However, with all that taken into account, I loved my work at the seminary. I was in the center of the institution that had changed my life, had given me a sense of hope and peace, had given me a shot at the finest theological education known to mortal man. I had a chance to make a contribution to the school that had given me more than enough, more than was required. I had a chance to help other students get in touch with our resources. I worked with gusto and with fulfillment. I had already begun to imagine how I would look at age sixty-five being presented in my last chapel appearance as a staff member of the hallowed haven of parson-preparation.

Then I met Bill Lancaster . . .

Bill and I were together for a conference for college students in June of 1966. In a week's time, we became good friends, more than casual acquaintances. He called me in July to see if I could come to his church to speak for a dinner meeting for the students coming into his community for the new year, and I accepted. It was to be in September of 1966.

The church was First Baptist in Decatur, Georgia, in the greater-Atlanta complex. I arrived on a Sunday afternoon in time to speak for a dinner before the evening worship hour. The fellowship hall of the church was filled with four-passenger card tables and decked out with red-checked tablecloths, candles, pizza—pseudo-Italiano . . .

I entertained for about forty-five minutes at the dinner; then, I was introduced in the evening worship hour. Afterward, I spoke to the students back in the fellowship hall. When it was all over, I went home to spend the night at Bill's home. Good visit. Warm feelings. Deeper friendship.

Next morning we fought Atlanta traffic in the rain to make a mid-morning flight to Nashville. We were bumper-to-bumper at one point, stalled, at a virtual standstill. Bill asked me in a most off-handed way my opinion of a mutual friend of ours who did some "all-over-the-country" type appearances, largely in churches. The person was talented, skilled, remarkably able in the area of music performance. I sat there in the rain, backed up in traffic, and began to respond out loud to my inclinations about the individual. In essence, I said that this person, in my humble opinion, had chosen to keep the gift in the church when the gift *also* had great potential on the concert stage, in opera, on Broadway. I felt that the gift had been squelched in many ways; I felt that the person was not letting the gift grow to its fullest potential.

Bill baited me. "I haven't known you long, but I know you well enough to believe I can shoot straight with you."

"Sure!" I replied. "What are you getting at?"

"I think you're doing the same thing!"

"What are you saying?" I hadn't the foggiest idea

what he was saying. Psychologists would say that my defense mechanisms were working overtime . . .

"I mean," he continued, "you are selling *your* gift short. You ought to be taking your talent for entertaining into other arenas than church basements! You could move around all over the country speaking to all kinds of folks, giving entertainment a shot in the arm with clean, wholesome humor. We need to get that kind of stuff in the mix of things, and you could do that. You really ought . . ."

By this time I was a bit numb and shocked. I didn't hear him well because I was resisting with all the strength I could muster. I had been licensed to the Baptist ministry when I was thirteen years old. I was an ordained minister now, employed by one of the denominational seminaries. I was right where God wanted me to be. Sure, I had been playing my ukulele all over the civilized world. I had spoken for every variety of church gathering and civic club known to man. I had been entertaining folks ever since I could hold my own with the storytellers at the Thanksgiving feed at my grandparents' home in Amarillo.

But entertainment had never been part of the game plan of my life. I had been called by God into the ministry.

By the time we reached the airport, Bill really had me in a tailspin. I thanked him and tickled the tummy of his son, Mark, to get one more giggle from him before I leaped on the Delta bird to Nashville. Bill and I stood on the curb for one more minute, and this was the pivotal moment . . .

I said to him, "Bill, when I said yes to the ministry, I said no to show business."

Then the sneaky rascal nailed me: "Did you ever

have a chance to say yes to show business?

Puzzled, I replied, "No . . ."

"Then," he said, "in my opinion if you've never had a chance to say yes, you've never really said no!"

I wore that statement like a leg cast for the next year.

It haunted me when I was alone. It took my mind on long walks in the middle of important meetings. It interrupted times of serious study and reflection. It caused me to sit in conversations without hearing the other half. I was having to face the honest appraisal of a good friend who made me look hard at my gift, my talent, and deal with it honestly.

In February of 1967 I visited New York and stayed one evening on the campus at Union Theological Seminary. I had dinner with two of our seminary faculty members who were on sabbatical leave there that year. The next day I went sight-seeing and sight-staring in New York City. I found myself in Rockefeller Center at the NBC Studios. I strolled in . . .

Some Lancaster-created curiosity got hold of my being that day, and I decided just to walk in and audition for the *Tonight Show*, to show Johnny Carson what he'd been missing. I didn't know the mechanics of such a proposal, but it was worth a try. I found their offices and attempted to schedule an audition. The secretary must have been amused at the ministerial variety trying to explain to her how he'd like his chance at the great *Tonight Show*. I was told then that they received over 2,000 applications *per week* from people wanting to get on the show. There was no way it could be arranged. She thanked me and showed me the door.

I wanted to call Lancaster and say, "You were

wrong! There is no room for me there! They turned me down!" You'd think they would want to help a person start at the top . . .

That left the tantalizing option at rest for several months. In July of 1967 I attended the American Alumni Council's annual meeting in San Francisco. On the opening night I was scheduled to do about fifteen minutes' worth of light entertainment during the awards dinner. On the same program, to conclude the evening, was Ralph Edwards, producer of *Truth or Consequences, This Is Your Life*, etc. I didn't even get to meet Ralph that night, though I was excited about appearing on the same platform with him.

I traveled back across the country with my family and arrived at the seminary a week later. On my desk was a letter from Ralph Edwards! I tore it open like it was a love letter on the war front.

He was most complimentary. He thanked me for my part on the program that night; he said that he had enjoyed my brief time very much. He said some other things that really sent me sailing around the halls for several days.

I sat down and wrote him back immediately, longhand. I thanked him for noticing, for writing, for being so gracious. I sent that letter off with great excitement. Three weeks later I received a second letter from him.

This letter indicated that he was producing a new talk show in Los Angeles and wanted to know if I ever got out to the West Coast. If so, he was eager to have me on his show as a guest. My head was really spinning. My poor brain was bonging. I could hardly finish reading the letter—my hand trembled so that you would have thought I was trying to fan up some air in a country church!

Why so excited? The day before, I had accepted an invitation to speak *in Portland, Oregon*! That's on the West Coast, friends!

I wrote him back, told him about my forthcoming trip to Portland, and asked if that were close enough to Hollywood to count. It was. On a Monday night in November of 1967, Ralph Edwards *himself* picked me up at the hotel to take me to dinner and then on to the studio where I was to make my first television guest appearance.

The show was called the *Woody Woodbury Show.* It was taped in Hollywood and shown in eighteen cities across the country. I didn't know that until Ralph picked me up at the hotel. I called Eleanor from the studio to tell her about the syndication of the show—that it was seen in several other cities. Then came a prophetic line: "I'm probably going to be discovered by somebody like Mike Douglas!" We both had a good laugh.

Mike Douglas did see the show in Philadelphia one month later.

Barbara Shotel, a talent coordinator on his staff, called me the day after he saw it. She said he had gone home after his show and found that his daughter had left the television on in the den. He walked over to turn it off. The *Woody Woodbury Show* was in progress and I happened to be telling a crazy story right at that moment. Mike sat down in his lounge chair and watched my entire segment. Barbara said he had then called her with the order: "Book Grady Nutt."

Barbara, along with a number of other folks, had never heard of Grady Nutt! But, she proceeded to call the Ralph Edwards offices until she located me. She reached me on Friday. On the next Wednesday, I was a guest on the *Mike Douglas Show*!

Over the next three years I was a guest on this show eleven times. It created a whole new dimension to my life. It helped me see the arena of entertainment as a place where I fit comfortably, where I belonged.

This enabled me to plan a move into professional entertainment as a career. That took about two years, during which time I continued to work at the seminary. The tugs and pulls of my speaking circuit played havoc with my work at the seminary and with my family time. Through all the complex feelings and opportunities and responsibilities, I continued to find a solid and confident sensation about a career as entertainer, minister, writer. In August of 1969 I left the seminary to embark on a whole new career, to be exactly where I needed and wanted to be.

And lo, another high moment! After ten years of "self-unemployment," I had a call from Bud Wingard. Bud and his "partner in crime," Tom Lutz, are two of the key writers for Hee Haw, the nationally syndicated and top-rated television show that has run longer than any other series in the history of the industry. They write all the jokes that aren't corny. They write about six jokes each year . . .

Bud had seen me once on the *Mike Douglas Show* several years ago. He was surprised to find someone from within the church having fun with church experiences. He and Tom wanted to talk with me about an idea of theirs which would involve some humor and "funning around" with church folks, customs, habits, quirks, etc. Could I come to Nashville for a conference?

Could I come to Nashville for a conference!

I went to Nashville for a conference! Out of that visit I had a chance to meet John Aylesworth and Frank Peppiatt, executive producers of Hee Haw.

Eventually, they invited me to join the cast as a regular member. It is a crazy, relaxed, and fun group. The feeling is "vintage family." I am allowed and encouraged to be myself. I love it. I am at home.

Bill Lancaster had turned out to be a prophet after all. He was in the right place at the right time saying the right thing to the right person. He helped me get ready to make the right decision. No new door ever opens to me that I do not take a moment on its threshold to say a prayer of thanks for Bill. He prepared me for the time when I would have a chance to say yes to show business!

And I said YES!

FATHERED ALONG

Grady C. Nutt. That's my dad! We have the same first and last names. Our middle names are different. Mine is *Lee*. His is a family secret . . .

He's made a habit of being bigger than I. He still is. I plan to let it stay that way! It was a handy fact when I was small and easy to intimidate by the rough-and-tough neighbor gang. I just reminded them that "my dad's bigger than your dad!" There was no question about that; so I stayed fairly safe.

Our relationship is warm and comfortable and fun. We share a deep love for each other and let it be known. I draw not only *strength* from that fact; I also draw *survival*! And I plan to let it stay that way!

It wasn't always so comfortable . . .

Dad was one of eight children—third from last. He grew up on a bleak farm in central Texas. He hit his teens just as the Great Depression hit the United States.

He grew up as a strong, large, hardworking young man. He had a huge frame (I've teased him for years that his skeleton would weigh over 200 pounds!), enormous hands and feet, uncommon strength/power. From pictures I've seen and from things I've been told, his father was an equally large and strong man.

Dad and I both had big fathers!

Most of all of what I know of his family background says that he was not raised with an abundance of tenderness. Bleak farmland, bleak times, bleak outlook all make for bleak families! He left home for good at age sixteen and found work in Amarillo, Texas.

A few quick jobs later, he wound up as a route salesman for a milk company in Amarillo. He sold milk to individual customers at first; later, he moved up to selling milk products to retail merchants— grocers, etc. He had a warm and natural wit, was a standout in any crowd because of his size and effervescence. He was a natural salesman, not a "con artist." He could point out the merit of his product, acknowledge your particular need, encourage you to consider seriously what he was selling, but never pressure you into doing something you should not or did not wish to do.

He told me once how to sell refrigerators to Eskimos. "Tell them if they keep their meat in there, it won't freeze!"

His fellow workers have told me stories about him that make me swell up with an uncommon pride. For instance, his best buddy, Nubbin Corn (true!), told me about Dad at about age eighteen. He could lift three-hundred pound blocks of ice from the loading dock at the dairy onto a large leather apron he wore on his back and carry the blocks to the truck!

(I also told the neighborhood toughs: "My dad can *lift* more than your dad!")

Working in Amarillo gave him the chance to meet

and marry one of the great women of the world, my mom, Doris Rickman. I probably owe most of my zany wit to Mother and her family. When they were passing out original issues of *funny*, Mother's family was on the front row with large baskets!

Dad moved rather rapidly through the ranks at the dairy, and it was not too long before he was the sales manager. However, his "title on the door did not rate a Bigelow on the floor!" He worked long and hard hours just to keep our heads above water. Fortunately, he loved his work and took great pride in his ability to understand all the different aspects of the milk producer's craft. He can still explain butterfat content in milk like a professor in an agricultural college!

We moved fairly often as I've already mentioned. As I look back on it all, our moves were not the moves associated with "moving up." We did not own a home until I was fifteen years old. My folks still live in it. Two bedrooms, one bathroom, small closets, tiny kitchen—paid for!

I've gone back to the houses of my past in Amarillo. Each time, my appreciation deepens for the struggles of my parents in providing for us. Each time, the houses look smaller. When my sons were ten and twelve years old, I took them to Amarillo to see where I lived when I was their ages. I drove by each place slowly, pointed out the trees I climbed, basketball goals I shot at, schools I attended, homes of cranky neighbors, bus stops. Finally, I just stopped the car . . .

. . . and cried.

How many times Grady C. Nutt cried over the tough times of his life I will never know.

Dad is human and has many shortcomings. It was difficult for me to understand at times how he

managed to raise a perfect son! I have learned a
basic fact about him in my adult years that has made
our relationship what it is today—*he did the best he
knew to do*!

One thing he did not do well was to explain to us
how difficult life was for him. What I often saw as
temper was, I am now certain, nothing more than
exasperation with the lack of funds and the burden
of providing for the family. He expected each of us
children to know instinctively not to wish for or ask
for certain things. We thought in terms of bicycles,
basketballs, new tennis shoes; he thought in terms of
survival.

Dad "surrendered to preach" when I was fourteen.
He sold his dry cleaning business and moved to
Jacksonville, Texas, to attend a small Baptist college
to ready himself for the ministry. I have teased for
years about the fact that he had an "eighth-grade
education with a D average and quit at Christmas!"
He had not had the advantage of an adequate
education, but he made a stab at attending college in
a special program to prepare to preach and lead a
church. From where I am now, I still do not see how
he did it. The task of supporting a family of four
children, pastoring incredibly small churches, working
on a loading dock at a wholesale grocery firm, and
cleaning and blocking hats, was enormous. He
tackled it with total commitment.

Dad was never pastor of a church large enough to
pay him enough for gas money to get there! But he
gave it his best effort. Our old station wagon had
paneled sides and a canvas roof and pallets in the
folded-down backend for four sleepy kids to pile in
at 6:30 a.m. on Sunday for the long trip to places
like Martin's Prairie. We'd get home usually after
midnight on Sunday. Our dining room table was

Dad's study and business office. I have a hard time concentrating on study and writing if I am *alone* in a room; he had to contend with World War III at his elbow while trying to understand the meaning of "the shewbread on the altar" in the book of Deuteronomy!

I was firmly entrenched in the teens when my father became firmly entrenched in the ministry. It resulted in much tension and misunderstanding. I longed for nicer things, better education, chances to "get ahead." We flared up frequently; we argued considerably. We could get into an argument about the color blue. One good thing about Wayland Baptist College for me—it was 500 miles away!

The next several years were full of misunderstanding and unhappiness between us. Each of us had a full load of things that "bugged" us with each other. In 1963, on Father's Day evening, we aired years of feelings in a matter of hours.

I left for Louisville, for the Graefenburg Baptist Church, with a heavy heart. I thought our relationship was done in for good. I was not sure we would ever have anything to do with each other again. It was one of the longest years of my life . . .

The first week in May, just days before I graduated from the seminary, I received a letter from Mother. It was about the first correspondence between us in almost a year. She said that Dad had wanted her to write to ask me for the most direct route from Jacksonville to Lousivile—*he was bringing her and coming for my graduation from seminary*!

That visit literally changed my life!

They arrived in Louisville and called our apartment. I drove out to meet them and lead them over to our place. I got out of my car and walked toward their car. Dad got out and walked toward

me. I didn't know what to do or say. I was, for one
time in my life, without anything appropriate to utter.

I held out my hand to shake his "big 'un." He
walked past my handshake and into my arms,
holding me in his. We were at home away from the
house . . .

In telling you earlier about my relationship to
Samuel Southard, I mentioned a group that nailed
me one day in the seminary cafeteria about my
hostile humor. Much of my anxiety about my
relation to Dad, much of my frustration with life in
general, came out in hostile humor. The weekend
my dad came to Lousiville, I felt hate go down the
drain.

He told me something that Friday night that made
the transition possible.

Dad said that all my life he had loved me with all
his heart. He was proud of me. He knew that I
thought he *didn't* love me; however, he thought the
main hangup was that he couldn't tell me in ways
that I would accept. So he quit trying. What I heard
him say, finally, was that I mattered to him; he was
pleased with me; he loved me with all his heart. I
could now stop trying to earn his love. I already had
it!

I remember seeing a television commercial made
by Bill Cosby for the Peace Corps. He said
something like this:

"Maybe you are one of those folks whose parents
couldn't say, 'I love you.' What they said was things
like: 'Sit up straight.' 'Eat all your supper.' 'Be in by
nine.' That was just their way of saying, 'I love you.'

"Maybe you're not the kind of person who finds it
easy to say, 'I love you.' In the Peace Corps, you
could build a bridge; teach people to read; work in a
clinic; teach folks how to farm with modern
implements . . .

"The Peace Corps has a thousand ways for you to say, 'I love you,' *without getting caught!*"

My dad got caught saying, "I love you" when I was thirty years old!

What's it been like? How have we done? It wasn't an overnight, fairy-tale episode where a kiss and a hug changed a warty ole frog into the handsome prince. It was rather like the biblical insight of Jesus about the mustard seed—it came slowly, but it is now so big and strong that birds can perch in the branches. *Parakeets or eagles!* We have our disagreements, but now we play them out against the backdrop of unquestioned love and affirmation.

Let me give you an example . . .

In the spring of 1969, I was wrestling very hard with the decision to leave my post on the staff of the seminary. I had firmly decided to move on to another post; it was an unshakeable conviction. Dad knew of my struggle.

In February I was speaking at Ouachita Baptist University for a Religious Emphasis Week. I was there for four days. One evening I received a message from Sherman Zimmerman, campus minister, that my wife had called and wanted me to phone home. I did. She told me that Dad had been trying to reach me. She thought he sounded a bit distressed and suggested that I try to get in touch with him.

I went to a pay telephone next to the motel on the main highway and called. He said that he had not heard from me about the job-change proposal, and he wanted to know what was going on. I told him I was going to leave the seminary but was not exactly sure what I was going to do. He said that he hated to see me leave the seminary; thought it was a good place for me. I thanked him for the affirmation, but I assured him it was time for me to go elsewhere.

He wanted to know if there might be anything he could do to help me with the decision. I thanked him for the concern and offer of help, but I also assured him that I had gotten in a habit of handling these kinds of decisions on my own. I said to him: "No offense, Big 'Un," (my pet name for him) "but I have just gotten used to doing this by myself."

Have you ever been hugged over the phone? I was that night. He said. "Son, remember all those years you needed me and I wasn't there? Well, this time, if there's anything I can do to help, would you let me try?"

I assured him I would. I told him I loved him. He told me he loved me. We hung up.

I stood in the booth and cried.

There had been a father-shaped void in my life for many years. There had been a son-shaped void in his. Between us, we have managed to fill each other up!

There just aren't any bigger dads than that . . .

AFTER-WORDS AND
ON-WORDS

When the pioneers reached Oregon after months on the Oregon Trail, their first thoughts and words upon seeing the grandeur of the new land must have been: "It was worth the trip!"

That's my feeling when I consider the ups and downs of my life. I stand to look back at all the confusion and doubt, all the love and support, and affirm that what I have learned has been worth the pain.

I have a minister friend who reminded me recently of an unusual statue. The statue is that of a boll weevil. It is located in the center of town in Enterprise, Alabama. The story behind the statue is a marvelous parable . . .

Years ago the farmers around Enterprise suffered two successive years of total wipe-out from the boll weevil. The cotton crop was devastated; the financial picture, the mere option for survival, was bleak indeed.

The boll weevil is to cotton what the tornado is to a mobile home park! It utterly lays waste. Farmers looked the possibility of a third year of weevil-evil in the face and did some hard thinking. Someone came up with the idea of planting peanuts instead. It was tried with astounding success. The town of Enterprise has become one of the world's leading peanut-producing centers and has enjoyed prosperity beyond the wildest dreams of the farmers who fought the weevil.

So they built a statue of the boll weevil right in the center of Enterprise, Alabama! The general feeling is that if it had not been for that demonic bug, they might still be blight-fighting. No one in Enterprise loves the boll weevil; they do not breed them for export; they do not enjoy hearing of the severe licks to the crops of other farmers in other places. However, they do realize that the weevil made them rethink their lives and their habits and their practices. Had it not been for the boll weevil, they probably would not be so well off today. And had it not been for my struggles, I would not be who I am today . . .

What kinds of lessons have I learned? What kind of fish were in my net when I hauled it in? What were my subtotals and inventory statements?

Several. I am a firm believer that when you sift the dust of your life you find an occasional nugget, gem, or treasure. Let me share some of the ones I have found.

ON RECEIVING THE BLESSING

I am convinced in retrospect that there is no more crucial need for a child than the parental blessing. Explore that with me.

In the Old Testament there is the story of Jacob on one occasion wrestling an angel all night. He was at the River Jabbok, camped on the edge of an uncertain future with growing dependents and pressing needs. All his life he had been the shyster, trickster, schemer, "hail fellow well met." This is a beautiful parable of a man coming to grips with the full blast of adult struggle. The angel is fought and held and set upon until Jacob finally receives his blessing. In his language, he was fighting for approval, for security, for abundance, for plenty. Many herds, much land, and a large family of sons assured him and all onlookers that he was indeed blessed of God.

A cloud of dust and a hearty bout on the bank wore the angel out first. Jacob had held on long enough to wrest the unquestioned favor of God from the messenger of God. He got a new name: *Israel.*

He also got a new problem. The angel touched him in the thigh and crippled him for life. Jacob was certain to have felt as he matured past the creek-bank pain that the blessing was well worth the wobble in his walk!

From that day on Jacob lent stability to the heritage of his people. He allowed others to drink deeply from the well of his humility. He both *sired* and *fired* his descendents with his process of becoming God's annointed.

The Old Testament concept of *blessing* has largely to do with material prosperity and good fortune. The family fortune accompanied the blessing of the father. There was also the unquestioned approval of the *blesser* that accompanied the *blessee* all the days of his life. My understanding of and need for "the blessing" comes from a growing awareness of the idea that every person needs to be welcomed into adulthood by his or her parent figures. We need to be affirmed by those who have readied us for life. We need to have our full and maturing personhood cheered and celebrated in meaningful and memorable ways . . . in specific ways!

I mention *parent figures* to encompass both our immediate family members—mothers and fathers, grandparents—and parent substitutes. Parent substitutes are those folks who stand in for our parents on occasions. Most of the people mentioned in this book are parent substitutes for me, especially Roy Flippo and Samuel Southard. All of these are resources and allies in the process of life. But they realize that there is a time when their role has shifted from *directing* life to *supporting* life for their now adult charges.

The family blessing is nothing you earn. It is given freely. You do not make Jacob wrestle with you before you give it. The prodigal son, star of Jesus' most poignant parable, came home from the far country smelling of hog lot, obvious battle casualty in the war of adulthood. He arrived in despair looking for a job. He knew he was not deserving of anything more than a hired hand's slot on the farm. He came home hoping for the *bunkhouse* and wound up in the *penthouse*! The family blessing allows for gross error, for stubborn independence, for repentance, for growing up.

I experienced my father's blessing for the first time at age thirty when he hugged me on a parking lot. I experienced it when he told me why he'd always had a difficult time relating to my demands and my personality. I experienced it when he, an adult, told me, an adult, about many of the things that had clogged up our relationship as adults. Many things he had shielded me from in my childhood and adolescence he now shared with warmth and trust. He included me in!

I received the blessing again when I joined the staff of the seminary. It was a marvelous experience. Men who had been my teachers and counselors were now my colleagues. On the first morning in my new post, I received two phone calls from professors. First, Harold Songer, then Morgan Patterson, called to take me for early coffee. Each of them told me virtually the same thing: "Now that you are on the staff and one of our colleagues, let's drop the *Doctor* stuff. Just call me *Harold.*" "Just call me *Morgan.*"

Just call me blessed . . .

The blessing needs to be verbal, symbolic, clear, direct, sincere. A child needs to hear that he or she can never sever the parent-child cord. In the event of a crisis, a bad decision, a "far country experience," the child needs to know specifically and feel with certainty that home is where to head! The parent's role is waiting and watching on the porch, with open arms, with "bandages and ointment ready."

I have been blessed . . . by many . . . in many ways. It has been my most cherished gift!

ON BEING AN AFFIRMER

Reviewing my life and "re-viewing" my life has made me joyfully and humbly aware of the affirmers.

In Roy B. Flippo—I first found someone who saw something special in me. He did not ask anyone else to give flannelgraph lessons at commencement. He did not ask anyone else to lead "Deep and Wide" (with motions). He obviously saw some gifts in me that he felt compelled and privileged to call forth.

In Hoyt Mulkey—I found a friend who tolerated the thin layer of maturity of a jeans-clad teenaged choir member (who didn't even belong to his church) long enough and often enough to lay hands on some strengths and focus them. I made myself available; I was hard to dodge. But he could have avoided me with some success. Instead, he chose to keep me close and to fan the glowing coal of my potential.

In Bill Lancaster—I found a person who said the hard word, the honest word, to a listener who wasn't listening very well! He made sure that I saw my gifts clearly and heard them declared with a note of appreciation and even wonder. He pressed me to make myself available for the "major league draft." He helped me to be ready for the first time I had a chance to say yes to show business!

In Ralph Edwards and in Mike Douglas—I found people established in their professions who took time to encourage someone on the way up. You will probably be interested to know that I have written Ralph Edwards many times over the past ten years and have never failed to hear from him by return mail. Air mail! His interest has bolstered me more than he can know.

Nothing gives me more peace in my own life than to take time to hear and encourage another person wrestling with his or her "angel," someone seeking the blessing, someone yearning for a place to belong. It is never a drain; it is always an investment.

Next to the blessing from our shapers, the most treasured gift is unsolicited affirmation.

ON BEING HONEST IN RELATIONSHIPS

At the writing of this book, both of my sons are young adults, college men. Both Perry and Toby have a quality that endears them to most of their friends—they are honest. Sometimes they are *painfully* honest! They are not manipulated by peer pressure like their dad was, and they do not thirst for approval as I did. Either of them, both of them, can tell another person precisely how he feels about virtually anything. And they often do.

I have always envied someone like that. Folks have asked me awkward questions all my life. Like: "How do you like my new haircut?" Or: 'What did you think of my performance?" I hate to hurt anyone with the kind of honesty that is sometimes negative and shocking. So, I usually find a way to cough and shuffle my feet and say something moderately close to the truth while keeping my very honest feelings successfully disguised.

I have been guilty of believing a misconception: *Honesty is the ability to say negative things.*

Did you ever think about this: "I love you," spoken from the heart, is very honest! "You did a superb job raking the lawn" is a cool breeze on the sweaty life of your young raker. And it's honest. Speaking the truth directly, affirming a trait in another individual, acknowledging a thoughtfulness on the part of someone else—this is honest.

When Perry and Toby were quite young and we were at Graefenburg, Kentucky, at the world's greatest country church, we were frequently invited to the homes of members for incredible edibles!

Farms have things like okra, squash, beets, and butter beans. Young boys don't always like those things. Some fathers, though ordained to the ministry, don't either!

We tried to encourage them to be honest with their hosts about the things they really liked and enjoyed about their meals. You shouldn't thank Mrs. Milton for fixing beets if you don't really like beets. Perry, our older son, hit on a great idea at about age five. He would get up from a piled-high table (piled high with many things he didn't care for) and say to the cook: "It was nice of you to have me for dinner." He thought that up on his own! It was thoughtful. It was almost clever.

And—very honest!

Samuel Southard made me face a major life issue when he riveted me to the floor with his comments about the lousy paper which I turned in—for a glorious 26! He told me in clear and simple language that I was clearly smitten with the simples if I didn't get my ability focused on academics. He refused to accept anything less than my best. He made me feel the same way about myself.

My dad unlocked the captive spirit of my life when he was able to verbalize his love for me and pride in me. I felt like a prospector half-a-mountain deep in a lost gold mine who had found the mother lode! (Or, should I say "father lode?") You could hear me through the mountain! I'm fairly sure he wishes he had said it sooner . . .

And, it has come to me in recent years that the ability to affirm a person with integrity and clarity makes it possible to confront a person with unpleasant or critical news. If I have spent years commending Eleanor for her beauty and her taste in clothes, it will be much easier for her to hear me say, "I really don't care for that skirt."

Important to remember: "I love you" is just as crucial in an honest relationship as "I disagree with you." And both can be quite honest!

ON SUPPORTING INDEPENDENCE

A valuable lesson I have learned in my life has to do with independence. Children ought not to have to earn it; it should be the trust fund made freely available by healthy parents.

This needs some elaboration . . .

Nearly every counselor, psychologist, pastor or psychiatrist I know—and I know several—will tell you that when you begin to "de-construct" a person's life, you spend most of your time getting at the places and areas in an individual's experience where parents failed or refused to let go. This can be intentional; it can be quite unintentional. Either way, it makes independence a brass ring that cannot be grabbed without high risk of falling off the happy horse on the merry-go-round!

Many well-meaning parents do serious emotional damage to their children by manipulating them into behavior, into vocations, into marriages which "are best for them." I am always romantically exhilarated by the idea of the prince choosing to marry the milkmaid, someone he truly loves, someone who meets his deepest needs and longings. Invariably, though, the king and queen take the crown back!

No gift given a child or student or parishioner is as valued or valuable as the gift of *initiated independence.* By that, I mean the conscious encouragement of the child's independence from the very outset of his or her life. There are certain decisions that are rightfully the child's to make, not the parents.

Eleanor and I had to deal with this at various stages, but nowhere was it more critically obvious than at the time the boys entered their teens. We had opened checking accounts for them at our bank. Then they were given their monthly "salary" which was to cover essentially all their needs. It was expressly stated that they were free to use the funds as they freely chose. I have rarely bitten my lip more often than I did while watching the parade of clothes they bought or did *not* buy, the records or bicycle tires or posters or black lights that came into the house. Having affirmed their freedom and right to choose, we fell into a new role with them. We were now challenged to learn to affirm the choices they made, to help them dig out of bad financial decisions, etc. We also had to deal with a very real parental dilemma: We had not given our sons real freedom if we had only given them freedom to do what we expected them to do!

Back to the parable of the prodigal for a moment. One of the overwhelming moments of sensitivity in the story comes when the loving father consents to the prodigal's departure for the far country, for "points unknown." Not for one moment do I doubt that the loving father spent many nights out behind the barn punching fence posts! You do not take hands off your beloved child, watch him walk into certain pain and disillusionment, without punching fence posts! That is what made him a loving father: *He granted his son the freedom to learn from his own mistakes and then loved him all the more when he made his own mistakes!*

There is a poster on the wall of my Sunday

School class that says: "God does not say, 'I love you *if* . . ., God says, I love you. *Period.*'"

That about says it all! But I have seen parents continue to place guilt and hurt and disappointment on their children in order to bend their wills and direct their lives. I have known middle-aged folks still controlled by parents who are retired!

Rhea Gray and Samuel Southard both knew of my hard times and failures, my sins and my disappointments. Each of them came back to me to offer me a post beside himself. Roy B. Flippo drove eighty-five miles one night to hear me speak for a Chamber of Commerce dinner in Friona, Texas. He was not delighted, I feel sure, with the direction my life had taken in my adult years. I know he would have preferred that I remain active in the ministry of Missionary Baptists and not in the Southern Baptist Convention. Nevertheless, he stood at the back of a long line of well-wishers and folks saying thanks to me in order to surprise me with his presence and to wrap me in his arms with a hug of love and affirmation. Not his to question, not his to disapprove. His to love me and let me know it.

My independence had been affirmed by each of my shapers. I can feel incredibly loved!

ON AFFIRMING THE PAST

If it be crucial for me to have my independence affirmed by my shapers, it is equally vital that I learn to affirm my heritage, my past, my pivotal characters. Not everything that happened in my past was good for me. However, many things are marvelous in review.

I felt it really fall into place in my life when Dad came to my seminary commencement. I have made mention of that two or three times already, but it is that much bedrock to me. What happened in the marathon sharing time I had with him that weekend was this: I learned that he had really and truly done what he thought was right; he had done what he thought was best; he had done the best he knew to do. When I saw past the misunderstandings and the stern discipline and the short temper and the clashes over virtually everything, I saw a father who could admit to weakness and inadequacy—and *love*. And I forgave all that was bad and embraced all that was good.

That was in May of 1964. And because of that encounter, in September of 1967 I could write Roy B. Flippo a letter. It was on the twentieth anniversary of his having licensed me to the ministry. I told him that I felt certain that there were many places where he and I were poles apart in our thinking, but I was certain that he was the most crucial influence for God and good in my life at that time in my life. I thanked him for all that was strong in our relationship, for all the love he had shown me, for the strength he had given me.

No one is able to mature enough to move ahead in life who has not been able to see with gratitude the gifts of his shapers and molders . . .

SO GOOD, SO FAR . . .

I am going to begin this final chapter in an unusual place . . . watching a soap opera.

I don't know its name. Wouldn't recognize it if you said it. I saw it in a motel room several years ago. It was an early afternoon. I checked into the room, turned on the air conditioner, pulled off my shoes, and turned on the television to see what kind of normal American family involvement Proctor had gambled on for the afternoon . . .

It was one of those pained expressions, organ-music-supported, grief with eye shadow. She was a young woman in her late twenties/early thirties. She was explaining the death of her husband (killed in a car wreck) to her niece—a girl of about twelve. The girl was having an angry bout with God and was telling her aunt about it! How could God do that to Uncle So-and-So? When she mentioned God, the minister in me sat up like a trained circus dog.

I was completely into this debate. I had watched television wrestling occasionally when we first had access to a set; so as a practiced veteran, I flinched, twisted, contorted, hurt, hit with every move on the screen. I was that much into this God-argument while lying on my motel bed, Dr. Pepper in hand, on that lazy afternoon.

The aunt reached a point where she knew that the girl was about to win. So she phoned her priest to see if there might be a chance that he could drop by to talk with them about the love of God and the death of Uncle So-and-So. He agreed to come by later. She hung up the phone. I was supercurious . . . Would the priest be able to convince her? Would the aunt's arguments be supported? Would the girl grow up to be an atheist? Would I have to tune in tomorrow . . .?

To my relief—and the aunt's!—the priest arrived shortly after the commercial. What would he do? What would he say?

It was masterful. He started by listening to the girl's anger. He knew, as most honest folks are aware, that anger is usually *hurt trying to get even*. He let her talk, encouraged her to "let it all happen." Patiently, he directed a line of questioning that set her to dealing with her own fears about death, about God. Then he did a beautiful thing . . .

Beside him on the sofa was a piece of needlepoint work the aunt had been using to occupy her own hurt. It was about half-way finished, rolled up a bit, needle stabbed through a patch of dark blue, thread hanging from the eye. As the priest talked with the girl, he slowly turned the needlepoint over and around in his hands. Then, he gently held it out toward her, bottom-side-up.

"Look at this for a moment . . ." he urged.

She took it in her hands and stared at the matted tangle of colored thread, hanging like disco-lit Spanish moss. The priest began to run his fingers through the threads and continued:

"On the back side of this needlepoint, you can't make out any particular pattern, you get no feeling for the picture being completed on the other side. But (and he turned it over) on this side, what a difference!" The camera and I zoomed in. It was a beautiful scene! (I don't remember what it was, but it was beautiful!) And from that point, he told a beautiful parable . . .

He showed her that life is often like a piece of needlepoint. On the underneath side of experience, from *our* perspective, it is impossible to make any sense out of the process—to get the big picture. However, on the top side, *God's* way of looking at life, there is a sense of unity and harmony. It reminded me of Enterprise, Alabama, and the boll weevil . . . a statue to a minus that became a plus . . .

The girl smiled faintly as he priested her into the awareness that her struggle would always be to learn to see the picture from God's perspective. He was able to use that piece of handwork to help her begin to feel that eventually the pieces would all fall into place . . .

I like much of the priest's idea in that moment. I march to his beat when he reveals that life is often an apparent mangled tangle of events and hurts and joys and loves and dislikes and confusion and certainties. At best, it is generally bittersweet.

I do not believe that God has some unquestioned pattern by which I must cut my life or you, yours. However, I learn daily that when I get a spiritual perspective on the tangles of my life, I see among the twisted threads the one that holds all the pearls! Like hearing Bubs Moseley explain negative exponents in high school algebra, I can suddenly say: "I get it!"

May I take this occasion to hold out as gently as the priest did the needlepoint an idea from the introduction of this book? I said then that the best idea of *witness* I have ever heard is "one beggar telling another beggar where he found bread!" You may find yourself recalling the words of a great hymn: "What more can he say than to you he hath said . . .?" Just a bit more.

And without sounding irreverent, it could easily be called "The Gospel According to Myself."

What do I see on the topside of my needlepoint? Is there scheme and purpose and direction and meaning? Yes. I do see through a glass darkly, but *I see through a glass!* Let me tell you about four glimpses of truth . . .

A SERIOUS VIEW OF HUMOR

Humor is my life. I know it when I see or hear it. I produce it. I vibrate to it. I understand it. Still, I find it difficult to explain. I think O. J. Simpson also has a difficult time explaining how he runs through the broken field in football.

Let me begin by making a strange statement. *Humor is not always funny.* It is usually clever and catchy and unhinged. It is sometimes wry and dry. It is often subtle. It can be penetrating and insightful. It is most usually bright and glowing. However, it does have a dark side to its moon . . .

Humor is at its roots *the capacity to describe*. It may be the description of a place, a person, a feeling, an event, an attitude. You hear humorous phrases every day: "Dark as midnight." "Slick as a whistle." "A puppy in the gnaw-it-all stage."

But, what about this one: "The gray in her hair was put there with the paintbrush of my misery."

Humor is the capacity to describe. It takes the tangible and uses it to picture—to parable—the intangible. "It is more difficult for a rich man to enter the kingdom of God than for a camel to go through the eye of a needle . . ." "How do you expect to get a splinter out of your neighbor's eye when you have a two-by-four hanging out of yours!" Jesus was called *teacher* more often than by any other title. Humor, parable, description were the basic tools of his trade.

Furthermore, humor is woven into the fabric of life just as surely as tragedy. There are tornadoes and murders and cancer. There are also surprise birthday parties, pranks, mispronunciation, chiggers, brushing your teeth with Brylcreem! In the midst of the awful is the absurd; in the process of frenzy there is boisterous laughter. Man causes Good Friday; then, God responds with Easter.

The humorist, therefore, is *interpreter*. One who uses *this* to show *that*. One who helps you see what he or she has seen, experience what he or she has experienced, feel what he or she has felt. It is only a short step from that to *minister* . . .

AN UNDERSTANDING OF MINISTRY

The soap opera priest summarizes minister and ministry for me quite beautifully.

He comes to the summons of hurt and bewilderment. He listens to the anguish and the questions. He acknowledges struggle without being judgmental. He did not bring with him a canned answer to the child's doubts and anger; instead, he found in the midst of the situation—the needlepoint—the vehicle readily acceptable by his young friend and her aunt by which he could convey his own understanding of the situation and of God's place in it all.

And President Carter illustrates graphically our difficulty in being ministers and understanding ministers. Let me try to make this "perfectly clear . . ."

It fascinated me when he became president that he brought his casual demeanor with him—jeans, flannel shirts, bare feet. I heard individuals remark that he was not upholding the dignity of the office. He was too "folksy." Some folks prefer cashews in the White House to peanuts . . .

And it became a parable for me. Folks were frequently offended by the fact that he did not fill the *role* of president in a manner generally accepted. Others appreciated in him the human qualities of ordinary folks. And they voted for him, and they elected him.

Ministers suffer from that same bizarre overexpectation. "I never knew ministers were funny." "I didn't know ministers liked jazz." "I didn't know ministers rode motorcycles!" Well, they do.

And they get lonely. And they doubt. And they fear. And they love. And they grieve. And they make mistakes. And they get divorced. And they have ulcers. They even enjoy sex.

If ministers have been *sinned against* at any one point, it is in the unreal expectations placed upon them by their parishioners, by their world in general. And here is my profound insight from all that: *Most folks want ministers to speak to them from their role, not from their humanity.*

And if ministers have sinned against their parishioners and their world at any one point, it is in trying to fulfill that expectation. "One beggar showing another beggar where he found bread . . ." The word is *confessional*.

That does not just mean that I face the congregation or church council and reveal my sin. It may include that. What that concept means is that I speak to life from my own life. I speak "but what I have seen and heard." I give my followers hope because I declare God's love out of my own struggle with sin and failure and hurt and joy and peace and laughter. I do not manage a sheepyard from the ninth floor of Stockman's National. I sleep under the stars with them and know their names and get cockleburrs out of their wool and care for them.

That understanding freed me from the burden of fulfilling a role. It allowed me to hear Bill Lancaster with my inner ear and heart. It put me in touch with my gifts and let me give away what has been given to me. It also let me hear a word from scripture: "Lose your life for My sake and you will find it."

That kind of loser never loses!

CHOOSING THE WILL OF GOD

I did say *choosing*. All my life I heard other terms: *finding* the will of God; *accepting* the will of God; *doing* the will of God; *surrendering* to the will of God. The last one was the classic encouragement— *surrendering*.

That has interesting overtones and/or undertones. You give up to God. You have been found out.

You are "arrested" by God, caught by God, programmed by God. *Surrendering* to God always gave me the hardest time in trying to understand Him.

My image of God came from a movie about Sergeant York—World War I hero who captured most of the German army singlehandedly, if you can believe the movies! I saw it as a boy and envied the hero. He marched about nine million German soldiers out of the woods with their hands on top of their funny-looking helmets with only his gun in their collective back. Hands up! You're finally caught.

That's how I felt about the will of God—you surrendered to it. In fact, the supreme calling was to *surrender* to preach! I have heard ministers actually say: "If you can do *anything* else and be happy, don't preach!" A great deal of the preaching I have heard was from ministers who surrendered to it instead of choosing it.

And that will need a bit of explaining . . .

I take seriously the fact that gifts and talents and abilities come from God. I cannot give heavy thought to the matter and grow an inch on my own; I cannot concentrate hard enough nor try long enough to have perfect pitch—the uncanny ability to hit a musical note without hearing it on an instrument first!

It follows, also, that I believe that gifts and talents are given with purpose. I would not be able to hear a perfect A-flat without hitting the piano if music were not in some way to be part of my life. Were I to be God, I would not endow you with a skill or talent or gift that I did not purposefully intend to be used and invested in the world. Nor would I call you to accomplish a mission or task for which you were not outfitted and equipped.

Let's get a bit "far out" about that for a second.

I have always known God would not call me to do certain things. For example, God will not call me to be a mother. God will not call me to be a professional boxer. God will not call me to be a jockey, an opera singer, or a ballerina. I couldn't do those things even if I surrendered!

But there are other things I must consider. I can entertain. I can preach. I relish photography. I have some flair for art and writing. I derive deep satisfaction from helping folks who struggle. These along with other gifts, talents, skills I may have are the ingredients God can use. I now open myself up to find direction and opportunity to invest all of myself where I can know the greatest joy.

I don't surrender to that. I *choose* that!

In the arena of your skills, talents, interests and gifts, you will find *always* the abilities to do what will bring you the greatest peace and fulfillment. And that is the will of God.

FROM HERE TO COMMUNITY

I have probably had as much community support and affirmation as any living human. If all the people who have loved me were placed in one room, you'd need a bigger room.

And most of them have been church folks. Long ago *church* ceased to be something I belonged to. It has become in every sense the drumbeat and rhythm of my life.

Hear now of vegetable soup . . .

This is a hypothetical situation—imaginary, not

real, and just purely thought up in my own headd.
For the sake of an argument and a parable, imagine
with me that my mother makes the world's worst
vegetable soup. Plays great piano, makes wretched
soup! (Remember, this is play-like . . .)

Most vegetable soup, you will probably already
know, is reddish in color, filled with a veritable
symphony of colors: green, yellow, orange, white,
red, and so forth . . .

My mother's soup is not that way. It is off-green. It
looks like avocado grits. It doesn't simmer like other
soups in the free world, turning the vegetables over
and over like slow-motion divers on *Wide World of
Sports.* Her soup lies there in the kettle like a mud-
pit at Yosemite, pursing its lips and poofing steam
and splatter . . .

You don't want this *on* you, much less *in* you!

I leave home and soup, finish college, and marry
a lovely woman, Eleanor, whom you've already met.
We have had three great weeks of marriage. I come
home for lunch every day from the church office.
Great lunches! Great marriage!

Alas, it was too good to be true! One day at lunch
she places before me a potion of unknown origin. It
has colored hunks in its reddish juice, simmering and
steaming before me in the wedding-gift pottery bowl.
I inquire: "What is that in yon bowl?"

"Soup," she replieth.

"Soup?" I shuddereth . . .

"Soup," she repeateth.

"What kind of soup?" I trembleth . . .

"Vegetable!" she celebrateth.

"Vegetable?" I cringeth!

"Vegetable!" she rejoiceth.

I am in great anguish. I had married for better, for
worse; I had married for richer, for poorer; I had

married for sickness, for health. Now, I had *worse,*
poorer, and *sickness* all at once!

She is beaming. I am shuddering. I think quickly.
(A humorist is supposed to be fast on his/her feet.)
What can I do? It comes to me . . .

"Dear, we have been married for three weeks
now."

"Yes, and it has been fulfilling," she twitters.

"And for me." (I really felt that way until lunch
today.)

"And I have asked every blessing at every meal, I
believe," I admit humbly.

"Yes, and you bless so well."

"Thank you, helpmate," I intone. "Today, though,
I wonder if you'd mind blessing our lunch."

"I'd be pleased, darling reverend," she sighs.

I am not going to bless something I am afraid of!

She starts thanking God for lunch. I start talking
hurriedly with my stomach . . .

"Stomach! Listen up!"

"Right! What's going on?"

"Just hush and listen. I really need your help!"

"Shoot . . ."

"I'm getting ready to send some stuff down there
and I need your cooperation!"

"What kind of stuff?" asks Stomach.

"Trust me!"

"Trust *you?* You who ate spaghetti with liverwurst
and Mountain Dew last night? Trust *you?*"

"Right! Trust me!"

"What are you sending down here?" There is
an eerie edge to Stomach's voice . . . a faint
rumbling . . .

"I am sending down some soup . . ."

"What kind of soup?"

"Trust me!"

"We've been through that! What kind of soup?!"

I swallow hard and whisper tentatively,
"Vegetable . . ." Soft . . . Shy . . . Fearful . . .

"*VEGETABLE*??" Volcanic! Defiant! Incredulous!

"VEGETABLE!!" I press on to bend Stomach's will
to my own. "And you will keep your mouth shut
and do as I tell you!"

I gain the upper hand! The moment is mine. I am
in charge!

"Amen."

"Grand blessing, darling."

"Thanks, sweetheart."

Now, to the task at hand. I eat about seventeen
crackers. You need to lay down a good base for this
next move. Then, I lay in a spoonful of juice—no
chunks yet. I chew as long as you can chew juice
without looking strange. Then, I toss it down . . .

I wait.

"What was that?" asks Stomach.

"Soup!" I reply.

"What kind of soup?"

"Vegetable."

"That's vegetable soup?" queries the chasm.

"Right."

"Hmm. Let's try that again."

I toss in another spoonful.

"Man, we've married a winner! Send down a few
chunks this time."

"Right."

Before long, the word is coming up repeatedly:
"More, more, more, more . . ."

Vegetable soup, particularly Eleanor's, has since
been our favorite.

From all that, a slice of meaning if you please:
*Most of us make the mistake of judging all soup by
the only soup we've ever known.*

I know folks who have had lousy soup at church. I know folks who have seen the church, like Rip Van Winkle, sleep through revolutions. I have known folks who experience church in shallow and legalistic ways. I know folks who hurt and never feel healing, who faint and are never comforted.

My word is: *I have found great soup in church.* I know from Roy B. Flippo and Rhea Gray and Sim Southard and Graefenburg Baptist Church and my sharing groups and my current congregation, the Crescent Hill Baptist Church in Louisville, Kentucky, compassion and worship and forgiveness and encouragement and love and hope and joy.

Out of that kind of community I have seen the meaning of faith take wing and soar. I have learned to believe in God and in myself. I have found marriage long after the wedding. I have the deepest friendships possible. I am more nearly a whole person.

SO GOOD, SO FAR . . .

It has been. It will continue to be, I feel sure. I am blessed with people who have loved me and continue to love me. I am at peace with my past and my heritage.

It is my deepest prayer and hope that you shall have learned a bit from my pivotal folk. There are others. These are symbolic, representative, and the most obvious. You will just as certainly have folks like them you will focus on and find ways to thank.

I close with a word of encouragement to you. I have been able to get to every single pivotal character in my memory and experience and say face-to-face those things for which I am grateful and upon which I have been able to build my life. Do yourself a favor and reap for yourself a thrill like you have seldom known: Sit down within the next week and write at least two such persons in your life a heartfelt word of gratitude. Be specific. Be honest. Be direct and to the point.

I can say confessionally and with the joy of humor in place, that because of *my* pivotal characters, it has been "so good, so far!"

And I can hardly wait for the next turn in the road . . .